£16-99
10/99

)

10

9

D0239653

"In working to develop new products, I find Dan Yankelovich's concept of dialogue wonderfully useful and practical. His depth of insight and years of data on the deeper trends in human values make him an unlimited asset to anyone who seeks to serve consumers in every culture."

—Craig Wynett, General Manager, Corporate New Ventures, Procter & Gamble

"The art of dialogue is becoming an indispensable management tool. This book shows ways of doing dialogue in a clear and cogent manner that managers will find invaluable."

—Charles M. Lillis, Chairman and CEO, MediaOne Group

"To innovate in any field today, the most urgent need is for dialogue to connect the silos of the mind. Daniel Yankelovich's dialogue helps experts from different fields connect various disciplines and functional professions. It lets us work together to create new ideas and products rather than for each to rub the other's ego the wrong way."

—T. George Harris, former editor-in-chief, *Harvard Business Review*; edited *Psychology Today* and *American Health*

"Dan Yankelovich has already advanced our understanding of what shapes public policy and attitudes with his book *Coming to Public Judgment*. As the rest of us were wrestling with how the 'working through' of an issue occurs, he has come to the rescue with *The Magic of Dialogue*. In it, he demonstrates how dialogue can facilitate the working through of an issue. Yankelovich not only describes the barriers to successful dialogue but also offers practical guidance on how to address the challenges posed when lack of skill or lack of will are present. His book is essential for people involved in business or public service."

—Horace A. Deets, Executive Director, AARP

"In this dynamic, global world where we have the war of the week, the trade negotiation of the week, the merger of the week, and the political crisis of the week, never has the need for dialogue been more apparent. The best managers and political leaders practice the kind of dialogue that Yankelovich describes in this easy-to-read and very informative book. Reading it will help them overcome conflicts and shape visions for the future that will win their followers full-hearted support."

—Pierson M. (Sandy) Grieve, former chairman and CEO, Ecolab, Inc.; partner, Palladium Equity Partners, LLC; Chairman, Carlson School of Management Board of Overseers, University of Minnesota

"Both practical and wise, this book distills Dan Yankelovich's vast experience into a set of guidelines and precepts, presented through vivid accounts of people encountering one another in talk. These are sometimes touching, funny and, yes, magical. Don't go into another meeting, any meeting, without having absorbed the counsel of this valuable book."

—Michael Schudson, professor, University of California at San Diego; author of *The Good Citizen*

"This book is really about a magic secret and that secret is dialogue.

"Dialogue, as it is reviewed and revealed by Daniel Yankelovich, is facilitator and inspirator. It can generate a leap of faith or a leap of imagination. It can produce far more than any participant brought to the conversation and that is its genius.

"No teacher, no member of government, no businessperson can afford not to read this marvelous little book with its big magic secret."

—Sidney Harman, founder and CEO, Harman International Industries

"I'm sorry this book wasn't available fifty years ago. Reading it is bound to improve your effectiveness as a manager as well as your personal relationships with your fellow men and women."

—Sol Price, founder, Price Club (age 83)

The Magic of
DIALOGUE

Transforming Conflict into Cooperation

Daniel Yankelovich

nb

NICHOLAS BREALEY
PUBLISHING

LONDON

First published in the UK by
Nicholas Brealey Publishing Limited in 1999

36 John Street	1163 E. Ogden Avenue, Suite 705-229
London	Naperville
WC1N 2AT, UK	IL 60563-8535, USA
Tel: +44 (0)171 430 0224	Tel: (888) BREALEY
Fax: +44 (0)171 404 8311	Fax: (630) 428 3442

http://www.nbrealey-books.com

© Daniel Yankelovich 1999
The right of Daniel Yankelovich to be identified as the author
of this work has been asserted in accordance with the Copy-
right, Designs and Patents Act 1988.

ISBN 1-85788-256-3 (Hardback)

British Library Cataloguing in Publication Data
A catalogue record for this book is available from the
British Library.

Printed in Finland by WSOY.

Contents

PART I

THE WILL TO DO IT

Why Dialogue Is Necessary

Chapter 1

Overcoming the Dialogue Deficit

Dialogue played a special role in reversing the nuclear arms race and ending the Cold War. Some years after the end of Ronald Reagan's presidency, George Shultz, who had been Reagan's secretary of state, asked Mikhail Gorbachev, former president of the Soviet Union, what the turning point in the Cold War had been.

"Reykjavík," Gorbachev answered unhesitatingly.

He explained that at their meeting in Reykjavík, Iceland, he and Ronald Reagan had for the first time entered into genuine dialogue with each other—a dialogue that extended far beyond their main agenda (arms control) to cover their values, assumptions, and aspirations for their two nations. Gorbachev credited this dialogue with establishing enough trust and mutual understanding to begin to reverse the nuclear arms race.[1]

In Oslo, Norway, in the year before Israel's prime minister, Yitzhak Rabin, was assassinated, a delegation of top-level Israelis and Palestinians, previously implacable enemies, held nonstop dialogue sessions over a period of months. Together they hammered out a blueprint for peace in the Middle East that lasted until Rabin's violent death upset the political balance.

These are history-making examples of dialogue. But dialogue is not the exclusive property of those who perform on the world stage. It works at all levels of life in ways large and small:

In San Diego County, a group of American and Mexican businesspeople and community leaders convene regularly under the auspices of San Diego Dialogue, a project of the University of California at San Diego (UCSD). These dialogues are so successful that once-intractable border and regional problems are now dealt with almost routinely.

In Silicon Valley, the CEO of a successful high-tech company recently held a weekend retreat with all the engineers in the company to conduct a dialogue on why so many of the most promising young engineers were leaving to go to competitors whose stock option plans were less generous than his own. After an initial stiffness, one after the other of the younger engineers explained that as much as they appreciated the generous stock bonuses, they felt that their ideas were unappreciated and brushed aside and that the employer reserved all of the important decisions to himself. One engineer said, "I know the stock options are supposed to make me feel like an owner, but when I come to work I don't feel like an owner. I feel like a peon, and that's not why I came to this company."

At first the employer (an engineer himself) was defensive in asserting his conviction that the CEO should be the undisputed leader who calls the shots. As the dialogue unfolded, however, he slowly began to qualify his position. Gradually, the session picked up momentum, with many of the young engineers offering ideas for improving the company's products and reducing costs.

By the end of the weekend, the employer had begun to re-examine his assumptions about leadership, and the engineers who worked for him had begun to understand him better. Subsequently, the employer made the effort to adopt a more consultative style of leadership. It never came naturally to him, but he saw the merit of it and was able to meet his coworkers halfway. Gradually, the flight of engineers from the company slowed to a trickle.

In Boston several years ago, under the auspices of the American Academy of Arts and Sciences, a number of Boston's public school teachers met over a several-day period with an equal number of professors from Harvard, MIT, and other universities in the Boston area. Together they carried out a sustained dialogue on how to improve public education in the Boston area. It was the first time these university professors (many of them distinguished scientists) and public school teachers had met as equals. Most left the meeting exhilarated and astonished at how much they had learned, how much respect they had developed for each other's point of view, and how much more hopeful they had become about future prospects for Boston's schools.

In a large midwestern food company, an older male executive formed a successful mentoring relationship with a younger woman executive. Both avoided any hint of sexual involvement and even the appearance of impropriety. A bond of real friendship as well as a business relationship united the two executives. Then one day a trivial misunderstanding triggered tension between them. The man wrongly assumed that he had offended his younger colleague's feminist sensibilities. An uncomfortable distance sprang up between them. Finally, however, they succeeded in engaging each other in dialogue. The misunderstanding evaporated as quickly as it had appeared. Now strengthened, the relationship resumed on a tranquil basis.

Every day countless dialogues—formal and informal, brief and prolonged, between strangers and between people intimate with each other—take place in a variety of settings and circumstances. Many, perhaps most, fail. But those that succeed transform people's relationships to one another, sometimes in ways that seem almost magical.

"The magic of dialogue."

I find the words easy to say now. Years ago they would have sounded exaggerated and unnatural to me. I would not even have known what they meant, let alone believed in them. Now they sound natural, and I fully believe in them.

The magic doesn't work if you substitute a different form of talk for dialogue. The magic of conversation? The magic of discussion? The magic of debate? None of these phrases rings true. But dialogue works its magic because it alone has unique capabilities other forms of talk do not possess.

In this book I identify what is special about dialogue, what gives it its magical properties, and, most important, what strategies individuals and organizations can use to help them conduct the kind of dialogue that best meets their objectives.

Most people have two purposes for doing dialogue: to strengthen personal relationships and to solve problems. Today, this second purpose is growing in importance: increasingly, we find ourselves facing problems that require more shared understanding with others than in the past.

The need to reach better mutual understanding through dialogue is strong in all sectors of society, but in none more than the business community. The growth of technology, the increase in the number of knowledge workers, and the blurring of boundaries of all kinds are transforming relationships at all levels of business. The traditional top-down style of leadership in a fortress-type company semi-isolated from others is increasingly out of vogue. It is being replaced by what I have come to think of as "relational leadership," where the defining task of leaders is developing webs of relationships with others rather than handing down visions, strategies, and plans as if they were commandments from the mountaintop.

Many forces converge to intensify the need for dialogue in business settings:

- The steady erosion of authority and hierarchy in the workplace in favor of flatter organizations.
- The trend toward forming strategic alliances with organizations that bring different corporate cultures, traditions, structures, and even languages to the new partnerships. Without dialogue, misunderstandings arise almost immediately.
- The need to repair the damage to morale that results from downsizing. Employers who have recently downsized or reengineered their companies confront a mistrusting and resentful workforce precisely when, to remain competitive, they need highly motivated workers.
- The need to stimulate the maximum amount of creativity, innovation, and initiative in coworkers, rather than simply expecting them to show up and obey orders.
- The need to align the entire organization in implementing shared visions and strategies.
- The growing demand by employees for quality-of-life benefits rather than exclusively financial and status incentives.
- The growing importance of developing a strong customer focus, which requires a better understanding of one's customers.

In this book, we will be concerned with dialogue in all walks of life: public and private, personal and impersonal. But I intend to give special attention to the requirements for dialogue in the business sector of our society and, by extension, to organizations that share the same sort of leadership challenges that business faces.

WHAT IS DIALOGUE?

What is dialogue, and what can it do for us that other ways of talking cannot?

Webster defines the purpose of dialogue as "seeking mutual understanding and harmony." In this book, I hew closely to the dictionary definition, straying from it in only one respect: I put less emphasis on harmony than the dictionary does, because the outcome of dialogue is not always harmony. In fact, as a consequence of dialogue you may come to understand why you disagree so vehemently with someone else; there will be better understanding but not necessarily more harmony.

In philosopher Martin Buber's classic work *I and Thou,* Buber suggests that in authentic dialogue something far deeper than ordinary conversation goes on. The I-Thou interaction implies a genuine openness of each to the concerns of the other. In such dialogue, "I" do not, while talking with you, selectively tune out views with which I disagree, nor do I busy myself marshaling arguments to rebut you while only half attending to what you have to say, nor do I seek to reinforce my own prejudices. Instead, I fully "take in" your viewpoint, engaging with it in the deepest sense of the term. You do likewise. Each of us internalizes the views of the other to enhance our mutual understanding.

To Buber we owe the stunning insight that, apart from its

obvious practical value (most problem solving demands mutual understanding), dialogue expresses an essential aspect of the human spirit. Buber knew that dialogue is a way of being. In Buber's philosophy, life itself is a form of meeting and dialogue is the "ridge"[2] on which we meet. In dialogue, we penetrate behind the polite superficialities and defenses in which we habitually armor ourselves. We listen and respond to one another with an authenticity that forges a bond between us.

In this sense, dialogue is a process of successful relationship building. Buber recognized that by performing the seemingly simple act of responding empathically to others and in turn being heard by them, we transcend the constricting confines of the self. Instead of saying "you or me," you hear yourself saying "you *and* me." The act of reaching beyond the self to relate to others in dialogue is a profound human yearning. If it were less commonplace, we would realize what a miracle it is.

Dialogue is not, however, an arcane and esoteric form of intellectual exercise that only the few can play. It is a practical, everyday tool accessible to us all. Nor is it a reversion to the participatory ideology of the 1960s with its insistence that everybody get involved in every decision, thus bringing decision making to a virtual halt. It is not, in fact, an instrument of decision making, which always involves considerations of power and interest—issues that interfere with dialogue. And it is not a negotiating device that seeks agreement leading to action. In fact, some of dialogue's most striking successes (for example, in our relations with the former Soviet Union) have occurred because dialogue preceded, and was sharply distinguished from, formal negotiations.

A MISSING SKILL

Until recently, most people made the assumption that no particular skill is required to do dialogue. They assumed that dialogue is just another form of conversation and that we surely know how to carry out conversations without requiring a special discipline. Therefore, there was little need felt for assistance in doing dialogue. But in the past decade, a growing literature has demonstrated that there is something unique about dialogue when it is done well.

Dialogue turns out to be a highly specialized form of discussion that imposes a rigorous discipline on the participants. If they fail to observe the discipline, they still derive the benefits of ordinary discussion, but they lose the benefits of successful dialogue. On the other hand, when dialogue is done skillfully, the results can be extraordinary: long-standing stereotypes dissolved, mistrust overcome, mutual understanding achieved, visions shaped and grounded in shared purpose, people previously at odds with one another aligned on objectives and strategies, new common ground discovered, new perspectives and insights gained, new levels of creativity stimulated, and bonds of community strengthened.

I do not want to overstate the benefits of dialogue. Though I believe it sometimes has almost magical properties, it is not a panacea for all the problems that ail us. Faith in the ability of talk to solve problems is very Western and, to some cynics, a sign of our cultural naïveté. It is certainly easy to poke fun at serious-minded and well-meaning attempts at dialogues that miscarry. And many efforts at dialogue do, unfortunately, miscarry.

Dialogue can fail for a variety of reasons. At times, violence, hate, and mistrust can prove stronger than the motivation to find common ground (as shown by, for example, Serbs and Albanians, Turks and Armenians, Arabs and Israelis). Or differences in interests can pose massive obstacles to dialogue. But the most frequent reason that dialogue fails is simply that it is not done well. Doing dialogue takes special skills that most Westerners do not yet possess.

This is because in the past there was less need for dialogue and therefore less pressure to develop the special skills it requires. Those in positions of authority—executives, teachers, parents—usually told others beneath them what to do without bothering to engage them in extensive dialogue. Much less emphasis was placed on mutual understanding. In schools, teachers exercised their authority without necessarily understanding their students' psyches or the wishes of their students' parents. In the workplace, employers and employees weren't expected to understand each other as one human being to another. The employer was the boss. If you wanted to keep your job, you followed orders and did what you were told. In smaller workplaces, personal relationships did, of course, develop, and people who worked closely together often did come to understand each other quite well. But the culture did not demand such mutual understanding. It certainly did not demand that bosses develop an in-depth understanding of their employees' attitudes, motivations, and sensibilities.

In traditional hierarchical arrangements, those at the top of the pecking order can afford to be casual about how well they understand those at lower levels. But when people are more equal, they are obliged to make a greater effort to understand each other. If no one is the undisputed boss anymore, and if all insist on having their views respected, it follows that peo-

ple *must* understand each other. You don't really have a voice
if those making the decisions aren't prepared to listen to you.

Today, cultural and legal changes mean that individuals expect and demand a voice in decisions that affect their lives,
and often they have the power to undermine those decisions if
they aren't allowed that voice.

Also, our society is becoming increasingly fragmented.
These days, individuals and groups divide themselves into
separate subcultures, like so many isolated silos on a field.
People identify themselves in terms of their own silo (e.g.,
profession, status, race, ethnicity, political loyalty), and they
develop their own special vocabularies, frameworks, values,
and convictions, making communication between these subculture silos difficult.

In the past, there was also far less pluralism. Today's diversity means not only that more people participate in decision
making but that the new players bring different backgrounds
and expectations to the table. Dialogue used to be simpler to
do because we shared frameworks. When frameworks are
held in common, there is no need to be self-conscious about
doing dialogue. No special method is needed to arrive at mutual understanding. You just do it—as naturally as you might
gossip with a neighbor or carry on any other form of conversation.

But we can no longer "just do it." Reaching mutual understanding through dialogue doesn't come naturally to us anymore. We cannot re-create the past conditions for doing
dialogue any more than we can re-create the small-town communities of an earlier era. In small pockets of the culture, ef-
fortless dialogue among people who think alike still does
exist—for example, between spouses in closely knit marriages
or among longtime colleagues who know each other's minds

and habits of thought so well that a glance, a shrug, a word is all that is needed to bring them onto the same wavelength. But the cohesiveness of people who have grown into a shared worldview through a long-enduring relationship is increasingly rare. It is becoming a thing of the past.

The special effort and discipline required to do dialogue skillfully in today's world are not widely recognized. When I told a friend I was writing a book on how to do dialogue, he was incredulous. "A whole book!" he exclaimed. "What's so difficult about doing dialogue? It's as simple as chewing gum. You can't write a book about how to chew gum!"

My friend's assertion that dialogue is as simple as chewing gum is dead wrong. Chewing gum *is* simple: it is both easy to understand and easy to do. Dialogue is neither easy to understand nor easy to do. It is, in fact, difficult to do well, and it isn't done well very often. If it were easy, dialogue would be flourishing in our society. But in fact, genuine dialogue between people who work together or share common concerns is exceedingly rare. At the present stage of our history, the ability to conduct dialogue is a marginal skill that only a tiny handful of people do well, a large number of organizations do poorly, and most people don't do at all because they do not recognize the need for it.

Here, to illustrate the point, are two examples. In the first, dialogue, had it been used, would have achieved an important institutional objective.

An Ivy League University

Several years ago, I conducted a study for one of America's most prestigious Ivy League universities on its future plans and strategies. Most of the faculty, alumni, and top administrators regard this university as one of the nation's great treasures. All expressed unstinting admiration for its president. But in my interviews with the deans of the university, one criticism kept recurring: all deplored the absence of a clear vision of the university's future.

I asked the president about the absence of a vision for the future. He stared at me quizzically for a long time. Then, without saying a word, he reached into his desk, pulled out a packet of papers, and handed them to me. Later, making my way through the packet, I found a series of the president's articles and speeches, all published in one or another of the university's many publications. Taken together, they expressed one of the most eloquent, coherent, and compelling visions I have ever encountered.

I then went back to the deans who had fretted most about the absence of a vision for the future of the university, and I asked them if they disagreed with the president's statements or found them wanting in other ways. They all reacted in roughly the same way. As one of them said, "Oh yes, I remember reading these when they first appeared. They are very good. I don't know why I forgot they existed."

The president's closest colleagues, the deans who manage all of the important parts of the university, had been expected to learn about his vision of the future *from reading articles he had written* rather than from the give-and-take of dialogue among equals that is needed to shape a *shared* vision of the future.

The president is an impressive thinker whose personal vision of the university's future proved to be farsighted, eloquently expressed, and passionately argued. While his statements were being formulated, the deans did not complain (very loudly) about the lack of dialogue. But the intensity of their feelings about being excluded from dialogue in the vision-shaping process was exquisitely reflected in their act of collective forgetfulness. Because they were excluded, the institution was left with an inoperable vision, one literally hidden away in a drawer. It was not a living, breathing, inspiring vision because the people who were responsible for implementing it were unaware of its very existence.

In the second example, dialogue is ideally suited to resolve an issue that is causing the company's CEO sleepless nights, but he is unaware of this resource.

A Biotech Company

The people most important to the future of many high-tech companies are not always found in the upper echelons of managers and vice presidents. Some of the younger, more gifted people at lower levels may not even be good managers, but they may be superb technologists with a masterly grasp of the company's work. The CEO of a dynamic biotech company in California calls them "knowledge practitioners." He says that they are the indispensable people in his company, and he freely admits that the hierarchy of his organization does not accurately reflect their talent. He is stymied by one of the most rigid rules of traditional hierarchies: you must not pay someone at a lower level more than you pay his or her manager. To do so is to violate the concept of advancement within a hierarchy: as you get promoted, your pay and status are supposed to increase relative to those left behind.

Giving gifted employees incentives that will retain their loyalty as well as their commitment to the work—without demoralizing their superiors—is far from easy. It is not solely a matter of money. For many knowledge practitioners, money is less important than it is for employees of traditional companies. In addition to money, what matters to many gifted techies are such mixed benefits as personal recognition, the quality of the primary education available for their children, flexible transportation arrangements, the right sorts of opportunities for their spouses, a sense of ownership and belonging in the company, and a stimulating place to work.

Dialogue among the various levels of management is an ideal method for working out the right kind of informal work contracts (balancing money and other benefits) for these new sorts of employees, who represent the wave of the future.

Our Western culture has developed many impressive skills. In some arenas, our know-how knows no bounds. We are remarkable in our ability to find technical fixes to problems. We know how to organize ourselves to do everything from lobbying for a traffic light on a dangerous street corner to fighting several wars simultaneously in remote parts of the globe. We know a lot about complex accounting, legislating laws, regulating industries, conducting scientific research, disseminating information, developing technologies, training professionals.

It is these and other gifts that make us so dynamic as a civilization. But among our most serious weaknesses is a surprising amateurishness in doing dialogue.

As skill in doing dialogue grows more widespread, I believe that the public will become as familiar with it as it now is with soccer and situation comedies. We need not all become experts at doing dialogue, but we ought to know the real thing when we see it, and we ought to be comfortable with it as leaders, citizens, executives, parents, lovers, professionals, and consumers.

My Personal Encounter with Dialogue

I am a practitioner of a fairly new profession that tracks social, political, and economic trends and measures shifts in people's values and beliefs. Why is a social scientist like myself writing a book on dialogue? Why is an outsider from an allied but different field seeking to make a distinctive contribution to people's understanding and practice of dialogue?

I believe the answers to these questions reveal something essential about the special nature of dialogue. It is not a coincidence that new insights about dialogue have come from people from a wide diversity of backgrounds and professions.

David Bohm, a theoretical physicist, is one of dialogue's most original thinkers. To his own surprise, he learned that world-class physicists develop their most creative ideas not in solitary thought (as the popular stereotype suggests) but through dialogue with one another. Martin Buber came to understand dialogue from his perspective as a scholar of Hebrew mysticism. His conception of the full dignity of the I-Thou relationship between individuals draws its inspiration from the dialogic relationship of people to God. Peter Senge and William Isaacs, two MIT scholars whose work I cite later in this book, are management gurus. They have discovered the distinctive contribution that dialogue makes to the success of business teams. Harold Saunders was a professional diplomat before he began to devote himself full-time to dialogue. Through personal experience, Saunders has seen dialogue succeed where diplomacy failed in finding common ground among longtime enemies (e.g., Arabs and Israelis, Russians and Afghans). Mikhail Bakhtin, an influential Russian social thinker and literary critic, has strikingly original insights into the role of dialogue in literature.

A physicist, a Hebrew philosopher, a Russian intellectual, a diplomat, two management theorists—it would be difficult to find a more diverse group of professionals. All of them have discovered something special about dialogue, and in each instance the discovery grew directly out of work in their own fields.

The same is true of my interest in dialogue. It, too, grew out of work in my own field. In conducting surveys to measure public attitudes and opinions, I stumbled upon a discovery about dialogue that greatly impressed me. It forced me to recognize that the way in which the public arrives at its most serious judgments runs counter to the conventional viewpoint. Convention holds that we gain our knowledge and understanding of issues primarily through factual information. The American political tradition has long maintained that an informed public is indispensable to the successful functioning of democracy. Thomas Jefferson held this conviction. The contemporary press holds it as an article of faith.

But is it really valid?

After decades of wrestling with this question, I have come to the conclusion that such faith is unjustified. The premise that the health of our democracy depends on a well-informed public is one of those unexamined pieties that professionals mouth without ever observing close-up how people really make the judgments on which our society does depend.

For instance, the United States is a prime example of a successfully functioning democracy. But it is not a prime example of a well-informed citizenry. I know this from my forty-plus years of experience in the field of public opinion research, and it is not exactly startling news to anybody who studies public opinion. It is certainly well known to the press—the chief drumbeaters for the importance of factual information. Indeed, the press delights in reporting poll findings that show how ignorant of the facts the public generally is (e.g., huge majorities of the public who can't name the chief justice of the Supreme Court or tell a Tutsi from a Hutu). Yet, on issues of fundamental importance to the future of our democracy, the public frequently arrives at judgments that are sound, considered, and sometimes profound. If an ill-informed public can reach sound judgments, some factor other than absorbing and analyzing factual information must be at work.

My research shows that the public's judgments are rarely the result of careful analysis of factual information. The public reaches its judgments through a different process than experts claim for themselves. Experts assert that their views are grounded on information, experience, and analysis. The public must be doing something different. The public is generally poorly informed, doesn't do much analysis, and on most policy issues has little direct experience.

The public, I have learned over the years, forms its judgments mainly through interactions with other people, through dialogue and discussion. People weigh what they hear from others against their own convictions. They compare notes with one another, they assess the views of others in terms of what makes sense to them, and, above all, they consult their feelings and their values. The public doesn't distinguish sharply between facts and values, as journalists and social scientists do. Indeed, dialogue draws heavily on feelings and values. Of course, information is important. But information stripped of feelings is not the royal road to public judgment; dialogue, rich in feelings and values, is.

Here we have one of the keys to why public judgment may be sound and mature, even wise, though ill informed. I have long suspected that something is seriously amiss in our conventional paradigm of knowledge, with its razor-sharp distinctions between "objective" facts and "subjective" values. In reaching its judgments through dialogue, the public is harking back to prescientific ways of knowing. These may actually have greater validity for the important questions of living together than current theories of knowledge do. (We will return to this theme later.)

It takes an extraordinary length of time for the public to arrive at considered and settled judgments. To return to the US, it took decades for Americans to decide that a committed internationalism, for all its drawbacks, was better than isolationism. It took decades for Americans to value freedom of the press so highly that they support the First Amendment even when they hate what they hear. It took decades for Americans to conclude that it was acceptable for women to work outside the home even if they did not have to do so for economic reasons. It took decades for Americans to decide that a woman, a Catholic, a Jew, or an African American would be acceptable as president of the United States. It took years for Americans to accept the victims of the AIDS virus as people worthy of help. It is taking years for Americans to come to judgment about the role of government in social legislation. (With the right kinds of dialogue and discussions, the process of arriving at considered judgments on complex issues can be dramatically accelerated.)

A very different kind of personal experience powerfully reinforced the lessons I learned about how the public arrives at its most important judgments. In recent years I have served on a number of boards of business corporations and not-for-profit organizations—about twenty in all. Such boards typically comprise a dozen or so members and are a superb mechanism for conducting dialogue. They meet regularly. They share common objectives. Their members are people from a wide variety of backgrounds who bring a diversity of experience to the governance and policies of their institutions.

Some of the boards I joined did not stimulate dialogue. The board of trustees of Brown University proved to be too large for intimate dialogue. CBS's board of directors conducted its meetings in a brisk manner that discouraged dialogue. Other boards, however, actively encouraged dialogue among their members. US West, one of the former Baby Bell companies, created an atmosphere in the early years of its existence that greatly encouraged dialogue among its directors. At the Kettering Foundation, the bulk of each trustees' meeting is devoted to dialogue between board and staff members on an issue of serious concern to the nation and to Kettering's programs. The board of the Educational Testing Service (ETS) always hurries to get its formal business out of the way so that its highly diverse members can engage in dialogue. Many of my examples of dialogue in the chapters that follow are drawn from my experience with these kinds of business and not-for-profit boards.

Serving on them gave me an insight into the striking similarity between their methods of arriving at judgments and the public's methods. Certainly, boards of directors representing formal organizations have better access to information and use it more systematically than the public does. But in the crunch, on the issues that really count, where the future of the institution is at stake (the kinds of issues with which boards are supposed to concern themselves), it is dialogue rather than factual analysis that most engages board members and shapes their judgments.

One brief example: ETS develops and administers standardized SAT and other tests that colleges and universities use for deciding who will be admitted and who rejected. These are high-stakes decisions that affect the lives of millions. A fundamental issue that ETS must confront is whether to continue to focus mainly on standardized tests (one size fits all) or to develop more customized individual assessments that will do justice to the wide variety of skills and forms of intelligence that young people bring to their studies.

From a business point of view, ETS must remain viable competitively. But ETS is chartered as a not-for-profit organization: its commitment is to enhance education, not to maximize its own profits. Its board is a heterogeneous one: some members are educators with little or no business experience, others are high-powered business executives. Some members are concerned primarily with equity in education, committed to making sure that minorities are treated fairly. Others are concerned primarily with excellence, committed to making sure that standards are maintained and improved.

Plenty of information exists about the strengths and limitations of standardized tests. ETS's board takes these facts into account. But the facts do not reveal to the board what its vision for the future should be or the best strategy for achieving it. Only high-quality dialogue among its diverse members and professional staff can yield this kind of understanding and judgment.

Every board of directors, whether of a profit or not-for-profit organization, faces comparable challenges. In my experience, the quality of the judgments these institutions make depends critically on their members' skill in dialogue.

PUTTING THE NEED FOR DIALOGUE INTO PERSPECTIVE

Sometimes words and concepts become fashionable for a brief time—words such as "empowerment," "quality circles," and "reengineering"—then quickly grow stale from overuse, to be replaced by other words that enjoy their own fifteen minutes of prominence before they too pass into oblivion. There is a danger that "dialogue" may share this fate and find its way into the graveyard of yesterday's platitudes even before it has a fair chance to show what it can contribute.

I do not think this will happen, for a particular reason. The need for dialogue is not a passing fad. My firm's tracking studies of the public, carried out annually since the 1960s, suggest that the need for dialogue is rooted in a fundamental existential condition of our society.

Many of the social bonds that once unified us as a people now appear to be eroding. Average Westerners, opinion polls show, suspect that their countries are growing apart. They sense that civility and respect for one another are losing ground. People feel that their dignity and sense of self-worth are being assaulted in countless ways, small and large.

An image that television has made familiar stays lodged in my mind. When TV programs on science portray our expanding universe, they show a picture of stars zooming further and further away from one another in the infinite expanse of space. This is the image I have of the drift in today's Western society: locked into our gated communities, our bigger cars, our smaller families, our professional silos, and our solitary selves, we are growing ever more isolated from one another. Increasingly, we worry that the ties that bind us together and unify us in our societies are loosening. We fear that we are becoming less closely bonded, more isolated, unglued.

How serious is this problem, and how great a threat does it pose to our culture? To keep the threat in perspective, I do not think we have reached the state of threatened chaos and loss that led the poet William Butler Yeats, in the aftermath of World War I, to write:

> *Things fall apart; the center cannot hold;*
> *Mere anarchy is loosed upon the world, . . .*
> *The best lack all conviction, while the worst*
> *Are full of passionate intensity.*[3]

Fortunately, something less fundamental is wrong with our culture. I detect no rottenness at the core, no deep decay of the sort that destroyed the great civilizations of the past. The center is holding; our world is not out of control.

These symptoms of a threat to our social cohesiveness can be interpreted in many ways, depending on one's standpoint. As a social scientist, I believe that we are confronting a manageable problem, not a fatal disease.

The problem is a growing "understanding gap." As a result of many trends converging at the same time, we are raising the bar on understanding one another. We demand much more mutual understanding than we ever did in the past. Yet, at the same time that we are expected to understand one another better, circumstances have conspired to place huge obstacles in the path of mutual understanding. We are gradually drifting away from one another. It is a disturbing irony that we expect higher levels of mutual understanding at the very moment in our history when our growing separateness makes such understanding so difficult to achieve.

We are becoming a society where impersonal, economic

transactions dominate. In a market economy, impersonal transactions are always important. Our society could not function without them. But increasingly, my firm's surveys of the public show that we crave something more satisfying to the spirit. We know that impersonal transactions cannot substitute for the deeper relationships for which people yearn, relationships based on mutual understanding.

The understanding gap has grown sufficiently threatening that it deserves to be addressed seriously. I believe that a certain kind of dialogue holds the key to creating greater cohesiveness among groups increasingly separated by differences in values, interests, status, politics, professional backgrounds, ethnicity, language, and convictions.

Fortunately, we are living in an era of enormous dynamism, creativity, and innovation. Perhaps more than ever before, we are willing to experiment and to adapt to change. Once the understanding gap is understood better than it is today, the energy, creativity, and will needed to close it will pour forth in abundance. When that happens, as it must, the skill needed to master the art of dialogue will become critical.

PART II

THE SKILL TO DO IT

Strategies for Dialogue

Chapter 2

What Makes Dialogue Unique?

On *NewsHour with Jim Lehrer,* the last few minutes are often devoted to a segment the producers describe as "A Dialogue with David Gergen" in which Mr. Gergen interviews someone currently in the US news. What distinguishes this segment from other television interviews is that Gergen's questions show that he has actually read the book or article the guest has written, thereby enabling him to make intelligent comments. This is a refreshing change from television as usual, but it is not "dialogue" in the sense that I and other practitioners use this term.

As I write these words, I have on my desk before me a number of books and articles with the word "dialogue" in their title. In most of them the reader would be hard put to distinguish these so-called dialogues from other forms of conversation. There is nothing that sets them apart. Some feature intelligent and insightful exchanges of views, but, once again, dialogue is used as a generic term to describe two people talking with each other.

If you ask a half-dozen people at random what dialogue is, you will get a half-dozen different answers. Until recently, even specialists did not distinguish dialogue from plain-vanilla conversation, discussion, debate, or other forms of talking together. Here and there isolated practitioners such as Martin Buber and Hannah Arendt saw special qualities in dialogue when done properly, but the concept remained alien to mainstream thought until the 1980s, when thinkers from a variety of fields began to rediscover its distinctive virtues.

Since then the topic of dialogue has gained astonishing momentum. In recent years more than two hundred independent community initiatives have brought groups normally isolated from one another together to address issues of concern to the community through dialogue. Organizations such as the Healthcare Forum have identified dialogue skills as essential to effective community leadership. At MIT, William N. Isaacs founded the Dialogue Project, dedicated to the practice of dialogue in the business community. There are dozens of similar projects and centers in the nation. Dialogue now crops up as an important subject in such diverse fields as leadership, management, philosophy, psychology, science, and religion.

UNSCRAMBLING THE FOUR DS

When specialists use "dialogue" in a highly precise fashion at the same time when most people don't bother to differentiate it from general conversation, the result is semantic confusion. One is never quite sure how the word is being used or what dialogue is.

My guess is that the semantic confusion will not last long. As the idea of dialogue catches on (as it is now doing), the need to clarify its meaning will grow apparent and its distinctive character will become more widely recognized. This has happened with other specialized forms of conversation. Reflect for a moment on jury deliberations, diplomatic negotiations, psychotherapy, conflict resolution panels, T-groups, quality circles, organizational teaming, board meetings, workshops, and conferences. Initially, all of these forms of talk were launched with only a vague idea of the special purposes they could serve. Yet all have now been codified and formalized in varying degrees in the interest of capturing their unique capabilities.

This has not yet happened with dialogue. Most people continue to use the Four Ds—Dialogue, Debate, Discussion, and Deliberation—interchangeably. This habit of speech makes the skill requirements of dialogue needlessly complicated. The skills needed for dialogue are not esoteric or arcane. Indeed, most are obvious, such as learning to listen more attentively. The complication lies in the confusion that must be cleared away before the skills can be addressed and mastered. It is as if the task were to erect a tent in a part of a forest covered with underbrush, old roots, and stumps of trees. Putting up the tent may be less onerous than clearing a space for it.

AREAS OF CONVERGENCE

Fortunately, there is a great deal of agreement among practitioners on how to distinguish dialogue from other forms of conversation. The most revealing distinctions are those that contrast *dialogue* with *debate* and *discussion*. (Deliberation—the fourth "D"—is a form of thought and reflection that can take place in any kind of conversation.)

Debate

All practitioners of dialogue emphasize that debate is the opposite of dialogue. The purpose of debate is to win an argument, to vanquish an opponent. Dialogue has very different purposes. It would be inconceivable to say that someone "won" or "lost" a dialogue. In dialogue, all participants win or lose together. It defeats the idea of dialogue to conceive of winning or losing. Those who practice dialogue have come to see that the worst possible way to advance mutual understanding is to win debating points at the expense of others.

Visualize a small group of neighbors, some of whom are liberal in their politics and others who are conservative, having a conversation about improving standards for schools. The conversation starts civilly. All have children in school and know how important education is for the future of their children. As neighbors they share a number of communal concerns, education being among the most important. They are searching for answers to difficult and troublesome questions.

Just as they are beginning to develop a common understanding of the obstacles schools face, one of the liberals in the group attacks the conservatives' endorsement of vouchers for school choice on the grounds that it undermines the tradition of public education in the United States. One of the conservatives in the group then responds by attacking a variety of liberal school reforms that, she argues, have sacrificed quality of performance in search of an unattainable ideal of equality.

A tone of hostility has now crept into the conversation. Those who have been attacked grow defensive. They marshal their arguments to beat down the opposition. They have stopped listening for understanding; they are now listening to detect soft spots in the others' positions so that they can controvert them. It all happens so quickly and automatically that no one notices that there has been a shift from conversation to debate. One thing is certain: no dialogue can take place.

The accompanying table is adapted from the writings of Mark Gerzon, one of our most gifted practitioners of dialogue. It contrasts the differences between debate and dialogue and shows how practitioners distinguish between these two forms of conversation.

DEBATE VERSUS DIALOGUE[1]

Debate	Dialogue
Assuming that there is a right answer and you have it	Assuming that many people have pieces of the answer and that together they can craft a solution
Combative: participants attempt to prove the other side wrong	Collaborative: participants work together toward common understanding
About winning	About exploring common ground
Listening to find flaws and make counterarguments	Listening to understand, find meaning and agreement
Defending assumptions as truth	Revealing assumptions for reevaluation
Critiquing the other side's position	Reexamining all positions
Defending one's own views against those of others	Admitting that others' thinking can improve on one's own

DEBATE VERSUS DIALOGUE *(continued)*

Debate	Dialogue
Searching for flaws and weaknesses in other positions	Searching for strengths and value in others' positions
Seeking a conclusion or vote that ratifies your position	Discovering new options, not seeking closure

Discussion

That debate is the opposite of dialogue is clear. Where discussion fits in is less clear—and more important. For it is in the distinction between discussion and dialogue that the distinctive quality of dialogue is best revealed.

It is useful to start with a *nondifference:* the erroneous assumption that serious conversation between two people is a dialogue but that if a larger group is involved it is a discussion. This artificial distinction mirrors a confusion about the literal meaning of the word "dialogue."

I recently came across a book titled *Carl Rogers: Dialogues.*[2] It presents a series of conversations the eminent psychologist held with outstanding scholars, including Martin Buber. Since the word "dialogue" is featured in the book's title and since some of the world's most noted practitioners of dialogue are involved, one would expect to find genuine dialogues. Clearly, that was the message the editors conveyed in the title they chose for the book.

I found the conversations between Dr. Rogers and others interesting and provocative but did not initially see why they were called dialogues. They were largely interviews that Dr. Rogers conducted in the presence of an audience, with Rogers interpolating his point of view from time to time (like the interviews David Gergen conducts with his guests on the *NewsHour*). The clue to why they were called dialogues came at the end of Dr. Rogers's interview with Martin Buber. In his concluding remarks, the moderator, Professor of Philosophy Maurice Friedman, said to the audience, "We are deeply indebted to Dr. Rogers and Dr. Buber for a unique dialogue. It was unique in my experience . . . because you (the audience) took part in a sort of *triologue* and adding me, a *quadralogue*"[3] (emphasis added).

Professor Friedman is making the common but mistaken assumption that dialogue literally means "two-sided." But dialogue has nothing to do with the number two. The word "dialogue" derives from two Greek words: *dia,* meaning "through" (as in the word "diaphanous," meaning "to show through") and *logos,* signifying "word" or "meaning." David Bohm, one of dialogue's most original practitioners, interprets its etymological roots as suggesting words and meanings flowing through from one participant to another. Emphatically, dialogue is not confined to conversations between two people. In fact, some writers on the subject believe that dialogue is best carried out in groups ranging from about a dozen to two dozen people.[4] It is ironic to see the word "dialogue" incorrectly used in describing a conversation between Rogers and Buber, both eminent theorists of dialogue.

What, then, is the difference between dialogue and discussion? Three distinctive features of dialogue differentiate it from discussion. When all three are present, conversation is transformed into dialogue. When any one or more of the three features are absent, it is discussion or some other form of talk, but it is not dialogue.

1. Equality and the absence of coercive influences. Practitioners agree that in dialogue all participants must be treated as equals. Outside the context of the dialogue, there may be large status differences. But in the dialogue itself, equality must reign. In genuine dialogue, there is no arm-twisting, no pulling of rank, no hint of sanctions for holding politically incorrect attitudes, no coercive influences of any sort, whether overt or indirect.

Subtle coercive influences are often present in discussion, and when they are they undermine equality and, hence, dialogue. The Rogers/Buber interview illustrates how nuances of inequality can creep into conversation. Carl Rogers claimed that he was able to engage his patients in genuine I-Thou dialogue because he empathized so totally with his patients' thoughts and feelings. But to the surprise of the audience, Buber rejected Rogers's inference. He pointed out that the relationship between Rogers and his patients is inherently unequal because patients come to Rogers looking for help but are, for their part, unable to offer comparable help to him. Under these conditions of inequality, Buber states, it is misleading to think that genuine dialogue can take place. What Buber calls dialogue between I and Thou cannot occur in the context of an unequal doctor-patient relationship. Therapy may be possible, but dialogue has nothing to do with therapy.

Mixing people of unequal status and authority does not necessarily preclude dialogue, but it makes it more difficult to achieve. Dialogue becomes possible only after trust has been built and the higher-ranking people have, for the occasion, removed their badges of authority and are participating as true equals. There must be mutual trust before participants of unequal status can open up honestly with one another. Buber did not maintain that Rogers could not engage in dialogue with people who happened to be his patients *outside* the therapeutic relationship (for example, on an issue of concern to the community); he simply said that dialogue was not possible within the constraints of the formal doctor-patient relationship.

People in positions of authority easily deceive themselves into thinking they are treating others as equals when they are not doing so. In the film *First Knight,* King Arthur is presented as a person of truly noble character. He proudly displays his Round Table, designed so that it lacks any special place of privilege at the head of the table for himself. He presents himself as just another knight among knights. Yet each time a decision is made at the Round Table, it is in fact Arthur who makes it or influences it unduly. There is no ambiguity about who the boss is. The Round Table may symbolize equality of standing, but the reality is otherwise.

A round table is an apt symbol for dialogue because it implies that dialogue cannot take place at the table except among equals. But as the film (inadvertently) makes clear, it takes more than a piece of furniture to create the kind of equality needed for dialogue to flourish.

2. Listening with empathy. Practitioners also agree that a second essential feature of dialogue is the ability of participants to respond with unreserved empathy to the views of others. In the example of neighbors discussing school standards, if both the liberals and the conservatives in the group were less eager to fight for their convictions and more eager to grasp the other's viewpoints, they might have been able to understand where their neighbors were coming from and why they felt the way they did.

The gift of empathy—the ability to think someone else's thoughts and feel someone else's feelings—is indispensable to dialogue. There can be discussion without participants responding empathically to one another, but then it is discussion, not dialogue. This is why discussion is more common than dialogue: people find it easy to express their opinions and to bat ideas back and forth with others, but most of the time they don't have either the motivation or the patience to respond empathically to opinions with which they may disagree or that they find uncongenial.

3. Bringing assumptions into the open. Theorists of dialogue also concur that, unlike discussion, dialogue must be concerned with bringing forth people's most deep-rooted assumptions. In dialogue, participants are encouraged to examine their own assumptions and those of other participants. And once these assumptions are in the open, they are not to be dismissed out of hand but considered with respect even when participants disagree with them.

For example, among black and white participants in discussions on subjects such as welfare reform, white participants sometimes make remarks that some of the black participants regard as racist. Most of the time, the black participants remain silent and do not respond, assuming that it would be futile to do so. Sometimes, however, one says something like "That sounds like a racist comment to me." The white person who made the comment will either bridle silently and resentfully or heatedly deny any racist intent. Either way, an unresolved tension has entered the discussion.

A genuine dialogue on this same issue would unfold in a different manner. Someone might ask the black participants if they thought particular comments had racist overtones and why. Participants could then ponder the answers without defensiveness. Or, once the accusation of racism had been made, judgment would be suspended and the group would focus on what assumptions people were bringing to the dialogue and how they judged whether or not a comment was racist. Once such assumptions are made explicit, disagreement may still exist, but the level of tension will be reduced and there will be better mutual understanding.

David Bohm emphasizes that our most ingrained thought patterns, operating at the tacit level, create many of the obstacles that isolate us from one another. Bohm stresses the link between people's assumptions and their sense of self. He is, in effect, saying, "When your deepest-rooted assumptions about who you are and what you deem most important in life are attacked, you react as if you are being attacked personally."[5]

Arguably, the most striking difference between discussion and dialogue is this process of bringing assumptions into the open while simultaneously suspending judgment. In discussion, participants usually stay away from people's innermost assumptions because to poke at them violates an unwritten rules of civility. If someone does raise them, they must expect to kick up a fuss or to tempt other participants to take offense or to close down and withdraw.

When in ordinary discussion sensitive assumptions are brought into the open, the atmosphere is likely to grow heated and uncomfortable. The discussion may or may not break down. It may later be recalled as a good or bad discussion, but—and this is the key point—it is not dialogue. The unique nature of dialogue requires that participants be uninhibited in bringing their own and other participants' assumptions into the open, where, within the safe confines of the dialogue, others can respond to them without challenging them or reacting to them judgmentally.

It takes practice and discipline to learn how to respond when touchy assumptions are brought into the open without feeling the need to rush to their defense and either swallow or ventilate the anger and anxiety we feel when others challenge our most cherished beliefs.

Think of assumptions as being "layered" (that is, assumptions exist behind assumptions behind assumptions). The more widely shared they are, the less subject they are to self-examination or to critique by others. Unexamined assumptions are a classic route to misunderstandings and errors of judgment. Dialogue is one of the very few methods of communication that permit people to bring them into the open and confront them in an effective manner.

STRATEGIES FOR DIALOGUE

We now come to the first of fifteen strategies. It is a bedrock strategy; without it dialogue does not exist.

STRATEGY

Check for the presence of all three core requirements of dialogue—equality, empathic listening, and surfacing assumptions nonjudgmentally—and learn how to introduce the missing ones.

In the chapters that follow, I will review a wide variety of successful dialogues. I will look at each from the point of view of what lessons they teach us about meeting these three core conditions and what added strategies they suggest. From this inventory of examples—some spontaneous, others carefully planned —I will abstract fourteen additional strategies for successful dialogue.

Chapter 3

The Billion-dollar Dialogue

I think of it as "the billion-dollar dialogue." It happened this way.

INVESTING OTHER PEOPLE'S MONEY

On most boards of directors, the choice of committee assignments is left to the preferences of the individual director. Most of the time I choose to serve on a company's pension committee. I do so out of a interest in investing and also because helping to ensure that people have a comfortable retirement is a socially useful act for a director to perform.

The pension funds of large multinational companies represent huge sums of money. The mandate of the pension committee is to make sure that when employees retire, the money needed to pay their pensions will be there, however long they may live after retirement. In performing their oversight function, the members of the pension committee must balance two goals that often conflict: investing the pension funds conservatively so as to preserve the capital the company needs to honor its commitments to its employees, and investing the funds boldly in order to increase the capital so as to counter unexpected setbacks such as a recession or a few years of losses.

It is not easy to balance these two objectives, and tension often arises between the committee and the professional managers who advise it and who do the actual investing. While the committee has the fiduciary responsibility for guarding the fund, it does not do the day-to-day investing. This is done by professional investment managers who work for independent firms unrelated to the company. Typically, these outside managers know much more about investing than the directors on the committee do.

Most pension committees meet quarterly. To these meetings, the committee invites one or more of the company's outside money managers to discuss investment strategies for the future. The outside money managers send their best salespeople and technicians to these meetings. With so much at stake, the men and women who represent their firms must know how to present their results, good or bad, with aplomb, patience, and sensitivity to the political climate. Typically, they offer their firm's advice to the committee in the form of highly technical charts that show in statistics the relative risks and rewards of alternative investment policies. For those not savvy about the technical aspects of investing, the charts are difficult to follow. The technicians the firm sends along with the salespeople are there to answer questions. But their answers are often more difficult to understand than the numbing statistics on the charts.

This approach, whether deliberate or not, has the chilling effect of reducing the number of questions that committee members might ask. It is hard to formulate cogent questions when you are unsure about what the numbers on the charts mean, and many committee members are reluctant to appear unsophisticated or slow on the uptake.

Most of the time, therefore, the committee members resign themselves to focusing on the bottom-line results. If they are good, the managers are allowed to stay on. If the results are mediocre or bad, the committee members begin to think about hiring new outside managers. This is a practical way of dealing with the problem, but it does not produce much enlightenment on either side.

As a result, discussions between committee members and the outside money managers are usually not very informative, and they almost never achieve the level of dialogue because none of the conditions for dialogue are present. There is neither equality nor empathy, and it is rare under these circumstances to bring fundamental assumptions into the open where they can be thoughtfully deliberated.

Yet every now and then a breakthrough occurs and dialogue happens despite all obstacles. One such dialogue focused on the question of business risk. The company's pension fund was huge: it had passed the $10 billion mark and the company had obligations to tens of thousands of employees. Despite its size, it was fully funded by only the narrowest of margins. Most committee members believed that the company's investment policies were too timid, especially since the company was facing several years of severe competition when every penny of added costs would count.

Those of us on the committee kept asking the outside money managers about the risks of a bolder investment policy, and they kept showing us charts demonstrating that our present investments represented, in their words, the "ideal balance between risk and reward." All of us agreed that the company's money must be invested prudently because we were playing not with our own money but with the financial security of the company's employees. No director wanted to jeopardize that trust. Yet we were frustrated, feeling that we had not achieved the optimum balance between conservatism and boldness. The outside firm, and even some of the committee's own members, argued that a bolder policy would entail an unacceptable level of risk.

As the discussion unfolded, one of our committee members, looking bewildered, asked the outside money managers how they could plot risk-reward ratios mathematically on their charts when in his experience he had never encountered risks so predictable that they could be reduced to precise numbers. One of the outside money managers explained patiently that it was the custom of the stock market to use market volatility as a proxy for risk (the more volatile the price of the stock, the greater the risk). He explained that it was therefore possible to get very precise numbers since the volatility of stocks and bonds can easily be quantified.

Most of the committee members knew this and were a little embarrassed to have one of their own display such naïveté. Nonetheless, the director's question launched a useful discussion about how much and what sorts of risk were appropriate to our employees' pension fund and our type of business. Gradually, the money managers grew less formal and instead of putting their energy into defending their firm's position began to participate wholeheartedly in the discussion. All of us focused our attention on when volatility was a useful marker for risk and when it wasn't.

One assumption after the other about the nature of business risk and how to take it into account in making investment decisions was brought into the open. Members of the committee explained certain realities about the nature of the company's business that the money managers did not know, and the money managers brought their wide range of experience with other businesses into the conversation.

Both sides grew more informal. They began to talk to each other as equals and to strain to understand each other's points of view. The discussion gradually evolved into a real dialogue that produced a greatly expanded area of mutual understanding. The meeting ended inconclusively, without any change in policy but with both sides feeling that something useful had been accomplished.

Several weeks later, the outside money managers requested a special meeting of the pension committee to which they sent their senior partners and strategists. At the meeting, they recommended a radical shift in investment policy. One of the partners explained the change: "When our colleagues came back from the last meeting with you," he said, "they recounted your discussion of risk and whether we were using the right proxy for calculating it. Since most of your employees are fairly young and won't retire for the next twenty years, the short-term volatility of the market is not a real risk. For your situation we need a very different measure of risk, even though we may not be able to plot it neatly on a chart. We have reviewed the kinds of risks your company faces in the future and have concluded that the real risks to your employees' pensions are greater following our 'conservative' approach than they would be if we shifted to a less conservative policy. We are therefore recommending that you make a substantial shift in your asset allocation from fixed-income investments to equities, despite their greater short-term volatility."

The committee accepted the recommendation and made the change. A year later, one of the committee members calculated that in that single year the change had gained the company's pension fund a billion dollars more than it would have had if the old policy had remained in place.

LESSONS TO BE LEARNED

In this section of the book, I examine two sorts of dialogues: those that evolve spontaneously from discussion and those that are planned in advance. I start with spontaneous dialogue because it raises fewer questions about process and format (e.g., "How many dialogue sessions should we have? Should we use a moderator? How long should each session last?"). These process/format questions don't become relevant until one understands what skills are needed for any sort of dialogue. I believe these skills are best exhibited in spontaneous dialogue, as illustrated in the example above. It is the lessons we abstract from this type of dialogue that will most help you as an individual get ready to take advantage of the many opportunities for dialogue that arise spontaneously every time you are engaged in a discussion.

What lessons and strategies can we abstract from this example?

Dialogue Has Tangible as Well as Intangible Consequences

It would be far too crude to claim that the difference between dialogue and discussion can always be measured in terms of money—in this case a cool billion dollars. In many instances, the consequences are intangible: more trust, closer bonds among participants, more mutual understanding, a better climate for doing business in. But as we shall see, the results can also be quite tangible, enabling people to achieve objectives important to their lives. And in instances of dialogue between old enemies, the payoff can be far more precious than money, preventing civil war, massive suffering, and death.

You Have to Make Dialogue Happen

In the eight years I served on the company's pension committee, we held more than thirty meetings with outside money managers. Many of them featured good and lively discussions. But this was the only one in which dialogue occurred.

In all the other meetings discussion did not evolve into dialogue, for a variety of reasons: The relationship of the outside money managers to the committee was one of consultant to client—an inherently unequal relationship. Also, the money managers and the committee members belonged to different subcultures, each with its own values, jargon, and framework. (From the outside, the business community may look homogeneous. But from the inside, every company, industry, and area of specialization creates its own subculture, contributing to the fragmentation that makes dialogue difficult.)

Perhaps the most important reason that dialogue failed to occur in all the other meetings was that it fell outside the unwritten terms of the transaction. The encounter between the board committee and the outside money managers was a straight business transaction. The managers earned their fee; the board members carried out their fiduciary responsibilities. In a business transaction you can buy discussion—intelligent, thoughtful, knowledgeable discussion. But you cannot buy dialogue.

Even in this one instance, the dialogue arose out of quite unpromising circumstances. Certainly, conditions of equality did not prevail at the beginning of the discussion: the board members were annoyed with the outside money managers and had the power to fire them at will. Nor was either side listening to the other with much empathy. For the longest time, the money managers stonewalled the directors in the interest of defending an investment policy they had pursued for years, and the directors, knowing they were being stonewalled, responded edgily and impatiently. No one was digging productively at assumptions until the one director happened to ask his "naive" but immensely revealing question about quantifying risk.

Giving Ground

One of the most useful lessons is that the dialogue did not begin until someone was willing to give ground. The dialogue started only when a director asked a question and one of the money managers was willing to suspend his commitment to his firm's "party line" to answer the question in a sympathetic and disinterested manner.

In other words, there were no clear signals in the discussion that dialogue could now commence, no pat formula, no tangible marker. The director asked his question in a friendly tone, breaking through a mood that had grown a trifle tense. He was genuinely curious about the answer, because he thought that perhaps the stock market had found some precise way of identifying and measuring business risk and he wanted to know what it was. The money manager who answered him responded to his question empathically. It is as if he momentarily stepped out of his role of defending his firm's official position and simply wanted to answer a good question.

This subtle change of tone turned the tide. Gradually, all the board members found themselves entering into the spirit of dialogue, as they had so often done in board meetings when outsiders were not present. Quite suddenly, all found themselves on the same side instead of on opposing sides.

Equality and Empathy Are Necessary but Not Sufficient

A fundamental lesson this example conveys is the key role played by bringing assumptions into the open. In the pension committee, enhancing the mood of equality and empathy created a warmer and more cordial atmosphere, but the dialogue didn't hit pay dirt until both sides realized they were operating on the basis of irrelevant assumptions (in that particular situation, about using volatility as a marker for risk).

It turned out to be fortunate that obsolete assumptions were identified and brought into the open and that the outsiders responded constructively. Things don't often work out with such spectacular success, because in an era of rapid change it is easy for obsolete assumptions, like computer viruses, to creep unsuspectingly into policies. Dialogue is uniquely well suited to bringing such assumptions to the surface.

Transactions Are Transformed into Relationships

This is a lesson that deeply impresses me personally. When dialogue happens, everything changes in intangible ways even though nothing may appear to change on the surface.

The most intangible change is the relationship of the participants to one another. In the pension committee dialogue, the participants became less guarded, less territorial, less manipulative. For the brief moment of dialogue, status differences disappeared. Participants found themselves responsive to one another in their common quest for understanding. The struggle to reconcile old assumptions with new conditions presented an intellectual challenge that truly engaged them. The visible product of the dialogue was a raised level of shared understanding. The invisible product was a relationship that went beyond the commercial transaction. As a result of the new understanding, important decisions were made and action taken—not in the framework of the dialogue itself but later, as a consequence of it. The two sides parted with an enhanced respect for each other and with a feeling of warmth.

Dialogue and Decision Making Do Not Mix

The final lesson we can draw from this example is probably the most important. I will come back to it in other examples because it seems counterintuitive and takes time to grasp fully. The lesson is the need to differentiate dialogue from decision making because the two processes demand such different disciplines.

In the example above, the dialogue and the decision to which it led were separated by a time interval of weeks, so it is easy to distinguish the two. In most examples decisions immediately follow dialogue. This is because once dialogue creates mutual understanding, the climate becomes conducive to decision making. Indeed, the most common purpose for initiating dialogue *is* decision making. Yet nothing ruins more promising dialogues and undermines more decisions than the failure to keep the two processes separate.

This example of spontaneous dialogue and the lessons it suggests leads us to two additional strategies.

STRATEGY

Focus on common interests, not divisive ones.

However homogeneous a dialogue group may be, each participant has his or her own interests to protect. In dialogue, it is better to seek common interests than to emphasize divergent ones. The outside money managers started by protecting their own interests: they were following the "party line" in justifying their earlier recommendations to their client. After the dialogue revealed that these were based on misleading assumptions, they had the wisdom to see that the interests they and their client shared were better for everyone to pursue than continuing to defend an indefensible position. It was a sound strategy.

STRATEGY

Keep dialogue and decision making compartmentalized.

Even when the sole purpose of a dialogue is to reach a decision, the dialogue part of the process should precede the decision-making part.

The line of demarcation between the two may be formal or informal, clear or vague, short or long. But the two must be kept separate or they will undermine each other. Most decisions do not, in fact, require dialogue because a high level of mutual understanding among the decision makers is not usually needed. But for truly difficult decisions, the act of seeking mutual understanding through dialogue should come before all of the practical constraints and clash of interests involved in practical decision making are brought to bear.

Chapter 4

Introducing Dialogue into Routine Meetings

The trustees of a prestigious research institute are attending a routine meeting, the first of four they hold each year. One item of business is to consider a replacement for one of their most popular faculty members, Professor Robertson, a biologist who is leaving to return to the University of California, where he had spent most of his teaching and research career before coming to the institute.

The trustees are sorry to see him go because he fills a unique role. Alone among the distinguished scientists on the faculty, he takes a personal interest in the young postdoctoral students who spend a year or two at the institute before moving (hopefully) to tenure-track positions at colleges and universities throughout the country.

These young scientists are at a vulnerable stage in their lives and careers. Most are single. Many have yet to find the project that will define their professional careers. The institute is isolated, they are alone, they have recently ended several grueling years getting their doctorates, and they feel unsettled. Professor Robertson nurtures them, gives them attention, helps them find projects, advises them about jobs, and in general gives them a helping hand during this tense transitional period of their lives.

The other senior scientists do not extend themselves in this manner. It is not that they are aloof and unreachable. Most are friendly and make it known that they are available if a young colleague has a specific question. But only Professor Robertson reaches out to give assistance without being asked to do so.

The director of the institute proposes to invite a famous biologist to fill Robertson's slot—a man who is almost certain to win the Nobel Prize in the future for his pioneering work but who is known as a loner, awkward and uncomfortable with people. He is a more prolific scientist than Robertson but a colder, less approachable human being.

Ordinarily, approving his appointment would be a routine matter: the trustees rarely question the recommendations of the director and his staff on faculty appointments. But on this occasion one trustee, an entrepreneur who has built a hugely successful high-tech business, raises the question of who will fill Robertson's unofficial role as mentor, friend, nurturer, and advocate for the many young postdocs at the institute.

His question launches a discussion of what the institute's role should be apart from scientific research, publication, and the advanced seminars for which the institute is famous. Opinion is divided, reflecting a split between the academic and business trustees: the academic trustees occupy high posts in universities as specialists in their fields, while the business trustees help fund the institute and keep its endowment and management healthy.

The academic trustees want the institute to focus sharply on its mission without distractions. They see no reason to question the new appointment on grounds of personality.

"We are not a nursery," says one of the physicists. "These young postdocs have to learn to swim or sink. We all went through it; why can't they?" Another says, "It is an open secret that Robertson's best work is behind him, so he is falling back on administration. That happens sometimes. That's why it is essential to invite only those scientists whose most productive period lies ahead of them."

The trustees from the business side are more reticent in expressing their views, but it is clear that something is troubling them. Finally one says, "Do you think that maybe we are encouraging the faculty to be too specialized and isolated? I've heard the institute criticized for failing to encourage cooperation between fields and even within fields. Maybe we are falling into the trap of knowing more and more about less and less and losing the big picture."

Other business trustees take up the same theme, a subject that has obviously been on their minds for some time. One is sharply critical of the institute for not encouraging more applied and interdisciplinary projects that cut across the academic disciplines.

Now it is the turn of the academic trustees to grow restive and twist in their seats. One observes that the universities and institutes that stress interdisciplinary work are among the most mediocre and unoriginal. In the politest possible language, another makes a comment implying that the business trustees are out of their depth and don't know what they are talking about. The atmosphere grows tense.

Then, in a self-confident and relaxed tone, a trustee from the business side (a highly successful publisher) comments dryly, "Those of us from business are all generalists," he notes, "so naturally we are uncomfortable with any kind of specialization. But that's what this institute is all about. It is the most highly specialized scientists at the institute who have made the real breakthroughs. So if we are uncomfortable, that's probably a sign that the institute is doing something right."

The trustees around the table laugh; the tension is broken. Now, in a more relaxed and less defensive manner, both groups of trustees continue the conversation, which has now unobtrusively evolved into dialogue. They listen to one another more attentively and reach out to understand one another. They trust one another more as equals. The university-based trustees feel less pressure to defend academic specialization; the business people become less critical. Each seeks the viewpoints of the others on the topics under consideration. Each makes his or her assumptions explicit (such as the assumption that generalists are uncomfortable with extreme specialization, however productive it may prove to be).

Gradually, two intertwined but separate themes are untangled from each other, and each is given the attention it requires. The question of how best to attend to the care and feeding of the young postdocs is teased apart from the more fundamental issue of the institute's long-term mission. It is agreed that whatever the institute's mission may be, more attention needs to be paid to the personal as well as professional needs of the younger postdoctoral scientists. Almost routinely, the new appointment is ratified, with the proviso that the institute set up a special board-faculty committee to devise new ways to attend to the human needs of the young postdocs, as distinct from their scientific training.

As to broadening the institute's mission, the trustees agree that the subject warrants more dialogue at a subsequent meeting, with much more preparation. The director states that he will launch a study to explore, both within the institute and outside it, the feasibility of greater integration across disciplines and the willingness of faculty within the institute to initiate interdisciplinary projects. One of the business trustees, well connected with research institutes across the world, volunteers to develop case histories of those who have ventured beyond specialization, with a view to learning from their experience.

LESSONS TO BE LEARNED

Many of the lessons we drew from the dialogue about business risk in the previous chapter are also applicable to this fragment of dialogue. Here, too, there is an unanticipated practical consequence: the care and feeding of the institute's postdocs will be approached differently than in the past. Here, too, a participant's tension-reducing comment is the turning point that helps to transform the discussion into dialogue. And here, too, the clash of subcultures proves a key obstacle to dialogue.

Even more clearly than in the business risk dialogue, we see the importance of cross-cultural communication. In the business risk dialogue, the encounter takes place between the subculture of professional money managers and that of corporate directors. In the institute dialogue, the encounter takes place between the subculture of academic-based scientists and that of successful business entrepreneurs. In the discussions leading up to both dialogues, the values of these two subcultures are gradually drawn into conflict with each other. In both meetings, the tone of the discussion remains civil but pointed. A palpable tension pervades both. Invisibly but inexorably, battle lines are drawn. In each instance, a participant decides to give ground in preference to confrontation, preventing the battle from escalating and instead deflecting it and turning it toward dialogue.

In the business risk case, overt confrontation would probably have been avoided because of the inequality factor. The outside money managers would have been loath to confront their client, and protocol would have prevented the board members from criticizing the outside firm in public; this sort of criticism would have come later, in the privacy of the committee's executive sessions.

In the institute case, however, the clash of cultures might easily have led to confrontation. The scientific and business members of the institute's board of trustees are on an equal footing. Neither group intimidates the other. Both groups are notoriously prideful. Successful entrepreneurs are a particularly prickly lot; the scientist's insinuation that they might be out of their depth in commenting on scientific research could easily have detonated a barrage of anger and criticism. I have seen it happen many times. Immensely successful people do not take kindly to public criticism of any sort, especially the implication that they don't know what they are talking about.

But when in the meeting one of the board's most successful business members decides to empathize with the scientists' concerns rather than take umbrage at the implied criticism, the tone of the meeting is transformed. The defensiveness of the scientists is quickly defused: the publisher readily acknowledges that the institute's commitment to specialization might be a reason for its success rather than a fatal flaw. The publisher's irony and graciousness also defuses the grumbling of the business members. The publisher's not-so-subtle message is "Let's try to understand each other's concerns rather than insist that our own concerns are the only legitimate ones." It is this message that prepares the ground for dialogue.

In both dialogues, the process of making assumptions explicit turned out to be all-important. In the business risk dialogue, it was hidden assumptions about short-term volatility as a marker for risk that made the participants realize that they might have been pursuing an erroneous policy. In the institute dialogue, it was hidden assumptions about the pros and cons of specialization that underlay the conflict between the two subcultures. The discussion evolved into dialogue only when one of the trustees broke out of his habitual framework, articulated his assumptions, and opened himself and his business colleagues to listening more attentively to what the scientists were trying to say. Though himself a generalist, through empathy with those who operate within the specialist framework he paved the way for the other business trustees to transcend their own parochial frameworks.

We begin to see why making assumptions explicit is so important. Doing so is one of the very few ways that one can build bridges between subcultures. By definition, subcultures are webs of shared values, beliefs, perceptions, customs, and styles. When two subcultures encounter each other on specific issues, misunderstanding is almost inevitable because there is never enough time or opportunity for each subculture to get to know and understand the folkways of the other. If the encounter between subcultures is for the purpose of getting something done of a practical nature, such as making policy decisions that affect the interests of both, one needs to find highly efficient ways to achieve mutual understanding. Making assumptions explicit is a highly efficient way, especially if a reservoir of goodwill exists on both sides. (In later chapters we will be looking at situations where mistrust rather than goodwill exists, making dialogue far more complicated. For most of us most of the time, however, the chief obstacle to dialogue is not mistrust but the increasing fragmentation of our society into subcultures without our having developed the dialogic skills needed to build bridges between them.)

These considerations lead to two additional strategies.

STRATEGY

Clarify assumptions that lead to subculture distortions.

Meetings of highly individualistic people have always had to contend with differences in outlook, values, and personality. Superimposed on these, however, we now have to contend with subculture differences as well.

It is always useful to identify the main subcultures represented in a meeting and to make the effort to understand their special idiosyncrasies and cognitive styles. (Businesspeople generally grow impatient if a meeting is disorderly, and they are embarrassed when strong emotion is betrayed. Academics like to point to the complexities of issues, even when these are not germane to action. Journalists fall easily into the habit of being critics rather than participants. The Japanese listen without participating. Engineers like to see issues charted in a systematic fashion. People from finance tend to force issues into a financial framework. And so on.) It would be gratuitous—and possibly offensive to participants—to call attention to these stylistic differences unless they are actively interfering with the stated purpose of the dialogue. Making assumptions explicit can be a touchy process. Even when done tactfully, the practice is not appreciated unless it is clearly relevant. When it is relevant, however, bringing assumptions into the open is one of the most powerful tools of the successful dialogist.

STRATEGY

Bring forth your own assumptions before speculating on those of others.

If you are willing to open up first, especially if what you say about your own assumptions shows you in a vulnerable light, it will make it easier for other participants to be equally open. Also, when you guess at what others are assuming, you risk having your guess interpreted as an act of aggression, especially if the assumption does not show the others in a complimentary light. It is acceptable for people to label their own assumptions as misguided or prejudiced: self-criticism maintains one's sense of honor and self-confidence. But being criticized by others does not. The publisher's admission that his personal preference for being a generalist might not apply to science was gracious as self-criticism. It might have been offensive if attributed to others.

In addition to their similarities, there are some differences between the two dialogues that add to our inventory of lessons and strategies. In the business risk dialogue, the central focus—finding the right investment policy for the pension fund—never changed. In the institute dialogue, the original focus of the meeting did change. It shifted from ratifying a new appointment to a concern with the goals of the institute. A subject of great import—the institute's mission—came up, uninvited, as a corollary to an issue of secondary importance in the overall scheme of the institute's life.

Often in meetings, the need to make a decision on a specific issue, sometimes an insignificant one, will bring an issue of far greater significance to the surface. After the larger issue has been ventilated, the original one becomes easier to resolve; it was difficult to resolve because it masked the larger issue.

This sort of shift in focus doesn't always lead from discussion to dialogue. But it can do so if participants want it to. One advantage of dialogue over discussion is that it is a superior way of building both mutual understanding *and* goodwill. Sometimes these are luxuries and not worth the extra effort of dialogue. But sometimes they are indispensable to accomplishing the task at hand. And they are always more satisfying to participants.

This consideration leads us to our next strategy.

STRATEGY

Use specific cases to raise general issues.

This, of course, is the strategy the US Supreme Court routinely follows. Instead of pronouncing on general principles in the abstract, it chooses the cases it will review on the basis of how well they embody the large issues with which the Court is concerned.

This strategy is precisely how most Americans bring their experiences and understanding to bear on issues. Most people do not have access to specialized knowledge. But they do have access to the beliefs, principles, and convictions they have acquired from their life experiences. They do not formulate these as abstract principles, as a moral philosopher might do. Rather, they apply them to specific issues, especially when these evoke the moral principles of fairness, justice, responsibility, integrity, and caring.

It is not surprising that the business trustees brought up the institute's raison d'être as a consequence of considering the specific issue of replacing a faculty member. Pointing to a specific case is an excellent way of focusing the attention of dialogue participants on important general issues.

In the last chapter I discussed the strategy of separating dialogue from decision making. As in the business risk dialogue, some of the most important of the institute's decisions (e.g., the role of interdisciplinary projects) were postponed to the future. The separation here was clear and definitive. Some decisions were made on the spot, for example, ratifying the new faculty appointment and deciding on a new approach to caring for postdocs. These decisions were the easy pickings, the dialogue's low-hanging fruits. All institute board members were in agreement about them, and methods of implementation did not concern them.

The larger policy issue about when to specialize and when to be a generalist in pursuit of the institute's goals was put off to the future, and rightly so. Making these sorts of decisions requires more than mutual understanding (the main benefit of dialogue). It also requires tough negotiation, and as we shall see, dialogue and negotiation are very different processes.

THE STRESSES OF MANAGED CARE

At their weekly management committee, the physicians and administrators of a prominent Houston hospital are reviewing a number of troublesome cases. One is the case of a patient who has been diagnosed with prostate cancer. The patient's wife wants to take him to a facility closer to their home for treatments. The hospital is resisting because, under its managed care contract, it will cost them extra money to comply with the wife's wishes. (Due to its own administrative error, the hospital had sent the patient to the wrong facility in the weeks before the diagnosis.) Because the hospital is having difficulty staying within its budget, the management committee decides to turn down the wife's request, despite the fact that the hospital itself made the mistake.

Just as they are preparing to move to the next case, the surgeon who had made the diagnosis, ordinarily a taciturn man, speaks up with barely controlled intensity of feeling. "Come on, now," he says. "This guy has just been diagnosed with cancer. He's depressed and frightened. He thinks he is going to die. Shouldn't we assume that our job is to take care of the patient and not just the budget?" This comment releases a flood of sympathetic reactions as the group wrestles with the conflicting demands imposed by their managed care contract and their own feelings and ethical tradition.

The other doctors begin to talk about the stress on their patients—and themselves—that the tight budgetary constraints impose. The meeting runs into overtime. Almost incidentally, the committee reverses its earlier decision and decides to honor the wife's request despite the extra costs to the hospital. As they leave the conference room, small clusters of physicians and administrators continue to talk heatedly about how the assumptions of managed care fail to fit with the assumptions that undergirded their work in earlier years.

Even though this example of dialogue is extremely fragmentary, we see reflected in it many of the same patterns as in the others.

It contains in miniature all three requirements of dialogue: The physicians and administrators treat each other as equals even though outside the meeting they represent a wide range of status positions. The surgeon responds empathically to his patient, and his empathy proves contagious, generating a comparable response in others. And in his outburst of feeling, the surgeon also makes explicit the conflicting assumptions about physicians' obligations under conditions of managed care.

The outcome of the dialogue has practical consequences, certainly for the patient with prostate cancer. A specific issue—the situation of one patient—precipitates a far more general issue: how physicians are to manage conflicting values. The specific issue gets resolved, and the decision reversed, when the larger issue is brought into the open and ventilated.

The articulation of an assumption is the turning point in the transition from discussion to dialogue. The discussion had led to refusing the patient's request. The dialogue reversed that decision and led to accepting the patient's request.

Several subcultures are represented in the meeting—but with an important difference. In our other examples, the subcultures were represented by different groups of people. In this example, the group as a whole has internalized the unresolved contradictions of the two subcultures (the traditional ethos of the physician versus the business ethos of managed costs).

This example leads to two added strategies.

STRATEGY

Focus on conflicts between value systems, not people.

In dialogue, one must be careful not to stereotype individuals by their subculture. Subcultures may also appear in the form of value systems in conflict within the same individual. In my years as a trustee and chairman of the Educational Testing Service, I found that the business trustees were as concerned with ETS's mandate to contribute to education as they were about its viability as a business; conversely, the trustees from the world of education were as concerned with the company's business soundness as with its commitment to education. As in the example above, two sets of values not two sets of trustees, were in conflict.

The best strategy is for participants to work with one another to bring conflicting value systems into the open, where they can be judged in the light of the specific issues the organization faces.

STRATEGY

When appropriate, express the emotions that accompany strongly held values.

One of our society's most deeply inbred assumptions is that objectivity demands that we keep facts and values (and the emotions that go with values) in separate compartments. We are supposed to be dispassionate about facts and keep our feelings at bay. In the example above, the surgeon did not do that.

Uncharacteristically, he spoke out with passion, turning the tide of the meeting. Had he said something general and abstract, such as "Let me remind you that our first obligation is to take care of the patient," it might not have had the same powerful impact on others as his impassioned evocation of the patient's state of mind.

Dialogue is never a mere technical or deliberative exercise. It always reaches into deep pockets of personal convictions and fundamental values. The expression of strong feeling may make the dialogue uncomfortable, but comfort is not its purpose. Quite the contrary, if the status quo is to be comfortably preserved, there may be no need for dialogue and discussion may be sufficient. But if change demands that the status quo be subject to question, strong feelings are bound to surface. It is usually better to confine the expression of strong feelings to the constraints of dialogue than open them to the randomness of discussion or the confrontation of debate.

Chapter 5

Transforming Casual Encounters Through Dialogue

Most dialogues do not take place in committees but arise spontaneously in an immense variety of encounters. These more informal encounters show dialogue in a different light than dialogue in meetings. Often they are more personal and revealing. In this chapter I report on four such dialogues—between two corporate CEOs, a teacher and a parent, a social worker and her client, and an older male manager who is mentor to a younger female manager.

The Old Bull and the Young Bull

The first example is a brief dialogue that helps to clear up a misunderstanding that threatens to wreck the personal and business relationship between two executives, a retiring CEO of a multinational communications company and his younger successor. The dialogue takes place on the morning after the old CEO's retirement dinner, where the new CEO, a close personal friend, made a moving speech that brought tears of appreciation to the older man's eyes.

Now, the morning after, the old CEO is chairing his last official meeting. Everyone in the room knows he faces his retirement with trepidation. A company man, he has no hobbies and no interests that compare in intensity with his dedication to his job. Everyone knows that the board of directors has turned down his request to postpone his retirement another two years, until he reaches age seventy-two. They had already granted him one postponement; they felt it unfair to his successor to give him another.

For weeks the retiring CEO has been hinting to his successor that he would like to be considered for a special assignment—to preside over a special ad hoc committee to review the future governance of the company. He now brings up the question of the committee assignment before the full meeting. An uneasy silence falls over the room. All present look toward the new CEO to hear his verdict. The new CEO suggests that they postpone the decision. Suspecting that the new CEO is resisting his appointment, the older man feels a spasm of angry resentment. He assumes that his old friend thinks he is over the hill and incapable of handling the job. Bitterly, he recalls his friend's gushing praise the night before and silently accuses him of hypocrisy and betrayal.

The younger man is nursing his own set of assumptions. He knows the retiring CEO has trouble letting go and suspects that he wants the governance committee job to maintain control from behind the scenes. He meant every word of praise he heaped on the retiring CEO the night before, but he has been waiting a long time to run his own show and feels he won't be able to do so if his former boss is constantly second-guessing him.

The meeting peters out in an atmosphere of tension. Everyone leaves the room except the old and new CEOs. Because they have worked together for so many years and have had such good rapport in the past, the old CEO swallows his bit-terness and asks, "Wayne, am I correct in assuming that you think I'm not up to the job of managing the governance com-mittee?" The new CEO bursts out laughing. "If you think that, you must think I am the world's biggest hypocrite."

The old CEO says dryly, "Something like that crossed my mind." His tone is calm, but he is still agitated inside, though Wayne's casual attitude has begun to reassure him. Sensing the older man's discomfort, Wayne puts his arm around his shoulders and says quietly, "No, Lewis, I don't think you are losing it. My fear is that you would do too good a job and I would never get a chance to run the show on my own terms. I need my chance to try out my own management style."

Now understanding, the old CEO says to his friend, "You were assuming that I can't let go and that I would be con-stantly getting in your way? Is that what your hesitancy was all about?"

"Bingo," says Wayne.

The tension slowly dissipates, and the old CEO admits, "I don't understand why, but I'm as anxious about this retire-ment as I've ever been about anything in my life. Frankly, the effect on you was the furthest thing from my mind."

"I know," says Wayne.

The rift has been healed. Objectively, not much has changed. The old CEO is still apprehensive about the future. The new CEO has yet to make up his mind about whether to give the older man the assignment he wants. But somehow everything has changed. The old CEO's self-confidence has been restored. His paranoia is gone. The new CEO sees the older man in a new light—as less daunting and more vulnera-ble than he had thought. The ultimate decision, whatever it may be, is now likely to be made for the right reasons.

*   *   *

This fragment of personal dialogue exhibits many of the lessons and strategies I brought forth in the last few chapters.

It shows, once again, that dialogue doesn't occur automatically; you have to make it happen. There is always some obstacle that needs to be addressed before dialogue can begin. In our other examples, the obstacle came from subculture conflict. That is not at issue here; both participants are immersed in the same subculture. Here the obstacle is that the preoccupations of the two men are miles apart. Each is focused on his own concerns. Here it is the difference in individual interests that gives rise to the assumptions that trigger the misunderstanding between them.

It doesn't really matter whether differences in interests or subcultures cause misunderstandings. In both instances, erroneous assumptions lead to misinterpretation of the motives and meanings of other people's actions and words. You may not be able to stop people from leaping to wrong conclusions, whatever the cause. But you can, with trust and goodwill, clarify misunderstandings through bringing assumptions into the open.

In their dialogue the two executives were able to draw on their long history of trust and goodwill. That is why the misunderstanding between them surfaced—and dissipated—so quickly. Without this history, the process would have taken much longer. But the dynamics would have been the same: first, someone needed to take the initiative and break the ice. The older man did this with his question. Then someone needed to be empathically responsive and to give ground. The younger man did this, once he recognized his old friend's anxiety and discomfort. Note that the back-and-forth between the two focused almost exclusively on assumptions—their own and each other's.

This example also illustrates the ability of dialogue to transform transactions into relationships. In this instance, a routine business transaction—a committee appointment—sidetracked a personal relationship. It was the older man's belief that the new CEO was treating his committee appointment solely as an arm's-length business transaction that enraged and frustrated him, especially in the light of the effusive tributes the younger man had paid him the evening before. The dialogue between the two put the transaction back into the perspective of their long relationship. In doing so, it was a profoundly healing experience for the older man. In effect, it gave him back the self-confidence that the prospect of an abrupt rupture with his life's work had undermined.

This episode also illustrates how a narrow issue can precipitate a much broader one. The narrow issue was a committee assignment. The assignment turned out to be highly charged emotionally: it involved both the older man's crisis of confidence and the younger man's concern with his ability to come into his own as CEO. The dialogue between the two men dealt with the broader issue, not the narrower one. But a decision still had to be made about the committee assignment. The new CEO was prudent to postpone the decision. The dialogue succeeded in dissipating its tense personal and emotional overtones, but many practical considerations of importance to the company remained to be resolved.

This episode leads us to a new strategy that the next two examples also suggest with even greater force.

A Gesture of Empathy

The next two fragments of dialogue, each between two women, underscore a strategy indispensable to initiating dialogue.

Parent and Teacher

The mother of a fourteen-year-old is in conference with her daughter's English teacher. The mother is nervous. She is not an assertive person, and she hates confrontation. She remembers her own reluctance when she was at school to have her parents complain to the teacher. But she feels she must urge her point. Her daughter has received a D in English, and she is afraid that it may jeopardize her future chances. Besides, the low grade was for spelling errors—in the mother's eyes, a trivial matter.

She explains to the teacher, "Susan has her heart set on becoming a doctor, Ms. Bishop. She will be taking premed courses like chemistry and biology in college, where spelling isn't that important. Besides, she's a techie, and she always uses the speller on the computer. That should cover most of the situations where good spelling is needed."

The teacher, sitting bolt upright in her chair and frowning, responds with a strong tone of annoyance: "Mrs. Kramer, they *all* use the computer speller. I explained to them at the very beginning of the year that I thought it was *terribly* important for them to know how to spell well enough for those inevitable occasions when they have to write something, say a note of condolence, and they cannot use a computer. I told them several times that I was going to grade for spelling. I don't want them to leave this school semiliterate and embarrassed." After a pause she adds, "Excuse me if I sound a wee bit querulous, but you are the fourth parent today who is upset about her child's English grade. I *was* a bit severe in my grading, but I felt I had to make a point of it."

There is a long pause in the conversation. Then Mrs. Kramer says, "Oh, God. What an ordeal it must be for you to have all of us parents barging in to complain, so sure *we* are right and the teacher is wrong. I wouldn't have done it if the stakes for Susan weren't so high."

Abruptly, the tension is dispelled. The teacher leans forward in her chair and smiles warmly. The mother's tension is also lifted. Soon she and the teacher are involved in a dialogue that leaves them both feeling better and that without changing Susan's English grade produces a strategy that will give Susan an opportunity to earn a better overall grade for the record.

It was an act of empathic listening that changed the trajectory of the conversation between parent and teacher. The parent responded to the teacher's lament by putting herself in the teacher's shoes, seeing the situation from the teacher's point of view. Grateful for the empathy, the teacher's attitude of weary hostility dissipated, and she in turn found it possible to empathize with the parent's dilemma.

Social Worker and Client

A social worker trained in the methods of Homebuilders (a US organization experimenting with new conceptions of social welfare professionalism) makes a call on a troubled client, a single-mother welfare recipient. The mother is harassed and almost beside herself with concern about her out-of-control teenage son. As soon as she sees the social worker, she turns away from her in frustration. "The one thing I don't need in my life," she says, "is one more social worker telling me what to do. Not with this house being such a mess. I need to get my house cleaned up."

Unruffled, the social worker responds matter-of-factly, "Do you want to start with the kitchen?" The social worker takes off her jacket, and without fuss the two women begin to work together to clean up the house.

Afterward, the two start a conversation that quickly

evolves into dialogue. By its conclusion, both women not only feel that they understand each other, but they also find time to discuss an action plan for the client to address her problem with her teenage son's acting out.[1]

This same social worker had a very different experience with her former employer, an agency that adhered to more traditional forms of social work. She recalls that in her first year with her old agency, she responded to another client in a similar fashion. She also helped her clean her house as a way to establish rapport and narrow the social distance between them. Then, too, she had positive results (which was why she is familiar and comfortable with the approach)—except that in the earlier instance, when she returned to her office and debriefed her colleagues, the more experienced social workers reacted to the incident with hostility. They told her angrily that her behavior was unprofessional. They said that in crossing the line to assist her client in doing her housework, she had made a blunder that, if generalized, would make their work virtually impossible. They argued that she was overpaid and overqualified to do that sort of housework, and in addition it violated her professional obligation not to get involved in the lives of her clients.

At the time she felt humiliated and confused. She left the agency after several unsuccessful efforts to engage the others in dialogue on how to reconcile their standards of professionalism with the need to establish the relationship of trust with clients that she felt was indispensable to their ability to give service.

In this example, the gap between the subculture of the social worker and that of the welfare recipient was more easily bridged than the gap between her and her former colleagues. Older and newer conceptions of professionalism in social welfare were driving a wedge between coworkers who appeared to belong to the same subculture but in fact did not.

The social worker was able to establish a base of trust with the client by a simple deed that demonstrated equality and empathy. Minimal trust with her coworkers was not established, however, with the familiar result of dialogue failure.

The lesson I draw from these examples is the importance of what I have come to think of as "a gesture of empathy." A gesture of empathy is probably the closest thing to an "open sesame" for dialogue. If in the heat of a discussion or debate you want to initiate a dialogue, your best chance lies in a gesture of empathy, especially if it is unexpected.

The teacher expected an argument from Susan's mother (that very day she had been involved in arguments with three other parents). Quite unexpectedly, however, instead of an argument, she heard Mrs. Kramer empathize with her while directing criticism at herself. The welfare client also expected an argument from the social worker. Instead, she received a simple offer of help—an offer that narrowed the social distance between them. The social worker's act of helping her client clean her house also makes the valuable point that you don't always need words to express empathy. It can also be expressed in action. When in the example of the two CEOs, the younger man put his arm around the older man's shoulders, that gesture underscored his words of empathy.

We therefore come to our ninth strategy.

STRATEGY

Initiate dialogue through a gesture of empathy.

The fact that gestures of empathy often come as a surprise tells us something about our society. In our transactions with one another, we are so used to wearing defensive armor that expressions of empathy are unexpected—and disarming. And since disarming is an indispensable prerequisite to dialogue, a gesture of empathy is the quickest and easiest way to start a dialogue.

Young Female Executive and Male Mentor

My final example in this chapter comes from a mentoring experience between an older male and a younger female executive. Mentoring relationships between older and younger men are a long-standing custom. Similar relationships between women executives are newer but also well established. But the idea of mentoring relationships between men and women in management is a more novel—and trickier—phenomenon.

As women increasingly move into the upper reaches of management, many are finding it possible to get the mentoring they need from older male executives, even though these relationships are always sensitive. Most of the publicity goes to their sexual overtones, but in practice men and women often deal with the sexual side of the relationship better than with the more mundane psychological aspects.

Here is a fragment of a dialogue that helped to solidify such a mentoring relationship.

Bob is the marketing VP of a large food company, and Audrey is the ad manager for the frozen vegetables division. She has been with the company since she received her MBA five years ago. Bob is more than twenty years older than Audrey, happily married, and the father of four boys. Audrey is recently married and is postponing having children until she is further along in her career. Bob sees himself in the young woman: her strong drive for success blends comfortably with her ease in dealing with people and her desire to please.

Over the past year, Bob has gone out of his way to help Audrey navigate her way through the maze of corporate politics and has also supplemented her training in advertising by giving her a better understanding of how to take other components of marketing such as distribution, packaging, and pricing into account. Audrey is a quick learner and grateful to Bob, whom she admires and talks about constantly to her husband, who, though not jealous, is bored with the subject of Bob and his virtues. Bob and Audrey have a comfortable relationship, with Audrey doing most of the teasing about Bob's choice of loud colors in shirts and ties.

One afternoon, Bob asks Audrey to pick up something for him the next morning at a store she passes on her drive to the office. She doesn't respond right away. Thinking she hasn't heard him, he repeats his request. She then says in a snippy tone of voice, "I heard you the first time." Bob feels a rush of irritation but says nothing.

On her way to the office the next day, Audrey does what Bob asked her to do, but both find themselves stiff and formal with each other.

Several days later, having coffee together while discussing a possible new ad campaign, Audrey says, "I'm sorry I snapped at you the other day."

Bob answers, "I wondered what was going on. It was so unlike you."

"I did pick up what you asked me to," Audrey says quietly. "You haven't said, 'Thank you.' "

"Then it's my turn to apologize," Bob says quickly. "I do thank you. It was thoughtful of you to do it, especially since you didn't want to."

"What makes you think I didn't want to?" she asked.

"Well," he said, "your reaction the other day. Clearly, I had asked you to do something you didn't want to do. You don't like to do personal errands for me. You probably find it sexist and demeaning. I don't blame you. I shouldn't have asked."

Audrey explains to Bob that she doesn't mind doing things for him at all. In fact, she is grateful for the opportunity to give something back. But she says she has always hated the feeling that she is being taken advantage of. Something about the way he had asked made her feel that way, and that was what she was reacting to, not any reluctance to do the errand.

He quickly denies that he was trying to take advantage of her, citing many reasons why that was not the case. She reassures him. Then she says, "I guess I was responding to you as I used to react to my father." She explains to Bob how hard she had always tried to please her father. "The more I did for him," she explained, "the more he expected me to do. It was some sort of game with him—to see how far he could push me. I don't mind doing things for people I care about. In fact, I enjoy it. But because I am so much that way, it's easy to take advantage of me. And when that happens, I feel resentful."

Bob admits how deeply irritated he had been when she snapped at him, even to the point of wondering whether the whole mentoring relationship was a stupid mistake on his part.

"Why didn't you say something?" Audrey asks, a little bewildered and hurt that a tiny episode could escalate so far.

Bob explains how his characteristic response to any rebuff is to withdraw into himself and not show how he feels. At times of tension, he pulls back, hiding his feelings rather than being open about them. He says he finds it easy to be open about "positive feelings" but not about anger and resentment (which he characterizes as "negative feelings").

Audrey observes that both of them have been making assumptions about each other that are not true.

This example illustrates a different sort of gesture of empathy: the apology. Most apologies *are* gestures of empathy; they express regret for offending someone else's feelings or concerns. Apologizing implies that you are aware of the feelings of another and can empathize sufficiently to regret having injured that person.

The example also adds to our understanding of why making assumptions explicit plays such a vital role in advancing the dynamics of dialogue. Most people are only dimly aware of how their past emotional experiences with others affect their current relationships. In the example above, it took several days for Audrey to become aware that she might have overreacted to Bob's request because it carried overtones of her relationship to her father. Whenever we overreact, the chances are that we are reacting less to the stimulus at hand than to previous experiences. The fury of the driver who goes berserk if someone beats him to a parking space is sparked by past frustrations that probably have a long history. All of us are constantly reacting to ghosts of the past.

In extreme cases, these ghosts can become more real than the present reality and the result is psychopathology. But even in normal, everyday life, we react to ghosts of the past. It can hardly be otherwise. We were not born yesterday. Our very identity is rooted in the accumulation of our experiences with other people and situations.

Audrey put a name (her father) on the ghost she was reacting to. Bob remained unaware of the series of ghosts past who had taught him to hide his anger and nurse his resentment without revealing any sign of it.

Psychologists use the word "transference" to describe this process of projecting onto others feelings originating in earlier experiences. The power of transference relationships is well known in fields such as psychotherapy. Indeed, dealing with the transference aspects of relationships is the very heart of the therapeutic process. This doesn't mean that psychotherapy has a monopoly on coping with transference; the process is too universal for that to be true. It does mean that the transference aspects of relationships probably cause more serious misunderstandings than any other source.

The subject of transference distortions brings us to our next strategy.

STRATEGY

Be sure trust exists before addressing transference distortions.

Transference is a universal phenomenon, an intrinsic part of human interaction. Most of us are only dimly conscious of its influence. Bringing into the open one's own assumptions and those of others in dialogue is one of the few ways we have to focus on transference-driven distortions.

But caution is advisable. In contrast to subculture distortions, transference distortions can get very personal. Subculture differences are far less personal. A teacher may place a higher value on spelling than a student or her parents, in keeping with the subcultures to which they both belong. Bringing out this kind of difference is not personally threatening to any of the parties involved. But bringing transference distortions into the open can be personally threatening and should be avoided unless a relationship of trust preexists the dialogue or is developed within it. (In later chapters, I will examine the important issue of building trust.)

APPLYING THE LESSONS

Before turning to planned dialogue in the next few chapters, let me summarize the salient points about spontaneous dialogue. Most of us will have more opportunity to engage in spontaneous than planned dialogue. If I am correct about the effects of greater fragmentation and pluralism on our society, we should expect to misunderstand each other more and more. Ordinary discussion is not powerful enough to break through these misunderstandings. We will increasingly need to resort to the more potent resources of dialogue. All of us will need to know how to initiate and carry out spontaneous dialogue, even if we do not get involved in the kinds of planned dialogue I elaborate on later.

Constant readiness is the key to success. You never know when an opportunity for spontaneous dialogue will arise. If you are not ready to take advantage of it, the opportunity will pass you by or, worse yet, you may get drawn into a dialogue that then turns sour, leaving the bad taste of failure in your mouth.

Constant readiness means that you are aware of all of the strategies we have been discussing and feel reasonably comfortable in applying the most important ones. For example, you understand the core requirements of dialogue: treating the other as an equal in every respect (as a "Thou" in Buber's sense of the term); being willing and able to listen empathically; and being willing and able to bring your assumptions and those of other participants into the open without becoming judgmental.

Should the need arise, you are psychologically prepared to perform a gesture of empathy without feeling that you are being too conciliatory. A gesture of empathy requires self-confidence and the lowering of defenses. If you are in full battle gear, as many of us are these days in our encounters with a self-absorbed world, it is easy to interpret a gesture of empathy as a loss of face, a deficit of macho, or injured pride. I suspect that most opportunities to initiate dialogue are lost because participants are not psychologically prepared to take this first critical step.

You must also be prepared to confront misunderstandings through focusing on assumptions. We have seen that misunderstandings arise from many sources: friction between subcultures, differences in interests, and, most complex of all, transference-driven distortions. Frequently these are interrelated. When you misunderstand people from other subcultures, you may be transferring to them attributes, feelings, and beliefs that are part of your own subculture. When you misunderstand people from within your own subculture, you may be transferring to them interests and feelings more appropriate to the ghosts of your past than to them.

Because dialogue is almost a lost art, few of us are ready for spontaneous dialogue. You can test your own readiness by asking yourself some searching questions. (You know your own strengths and vulnerabilities better than anyone else does.) Suppose, for example, you are an executive in a meeting attended by people of varied ranks within your organization—some who report to you, others who hold a higher position. A discussion is in progress regarding a project that did not work out according to plan. Lots of criticism is being bandied about. Are you prepared to volunteer that you accept some responsibility because of your erroneous assumptions and then make them explicit? If not, you may want to do more to prepare yourself for dialogue.

Or suppose you are a married man and you have just had a quarrel with your wife. You tell a friend, who then asks you, "After your quarrel, did your wife feel you had listened fully and sympathetically to her side of the story?" If your answer is "No" or "I'm not sure," chances are you are not quite ready to enter into dialogue with your wife.

Or suppose you are a woman with a younger sister whom you habitually treat as not quite equal to you in experience or smarts. Ask yourself if your attitude toward her reflects the person she is today or whether you are still reacting to her as she was in the past. To prepare yourself for dialogue with her, you may want to divest yourself of some of the baggage of the past.

One should not underestimate how difficult it is to break ingrained habits of not listening, to break through your wall of guarded reserve in order to offer acts of empathy, or to develop the skill of digging out your own and other people's assumptions in a nonjudgmental fashion.

Chapter 6

Planned Dialogue

One of the most common forms of planned dialogues is the corporate retreat, where groups of executives get away from their desks and phones to meet away from the office for one or several days. The purpose is usually to consider some longer-term or more fundamental aspect of the business.

Here is a typical example. The chairman and CEO of a large chemical company has brought a group of the company's top executives to a two-day retreat in the country to discuss the company's future. The chairman is widely respected for his financial acumen, but his colleagues do not feel close to him because he keeps his distance in his relationships with people.

Dressed casually in slacks and a red wool sweater, he starts the meeting by saying, "We are here at a difficult time in the company's history, and we won't get anywhere unless we are completely honest and open with each other in our dialogue together. I promise to do so, and I hope all of you will too. I want you to be as brutally frank and honest with me and my shortcomings as you would be if I were not present. This is a completely informal meeting."

A nervous laugh runs through the executives, most of whom greet the chairman's words with skepticism bordering on cynicism. They don't take him at his word, but the meeting proceeds smoothly anyway. For a day and a half, the talk is lively, yet no new perspectives emerge. The twenty-seven men and three women executives bring up familiar problems and familiar solutions. They remain in full armor. On the surface, the tone of the meeting is as informal as the dress code. But no one lets down his or her guard, even for an instant. The chairman is informal, friendly, asks intelligent questions, and makes perceptive observations. But nothing is accomplished that could not have been done more conveniently in the company's home office or even through e-mail.

Then, just before lunch on the second day of the retreat, something happens. It is a tiny incident, barely perceptible to an outside observer. But it transforms the dynamics of the meeting. The human resources VP is taking responsibility for having recommended a new head for the company's law department who messed up on the job and in fact has landed the company in a lawsuit. The chairman interrupts and says, "Warren, it is damn good of you to take the blame for that humongous mistake. But it is my fault, not yours. The man's reputation blinded me, and I didn't look deeply enough into his past record. There were plenty of signs of trouble, but I ignored them. Sometimes you just get carried away."

The conversation drifts on to another subject. Yet within minutes the executives begin to ask the chairman tough questions that have lurked beneath the surface from the outset but that no one has risked bringing into the open. The chairman responds as frankly as he had promised to at the beginning of the meeting. But no one believed him then. No one believed that he would really set status differences aside and treat everyone as equals. His willingness to admit to having made a serious mistake makes his pledge more credible. Once he drops his own armor, the others are willing to follow his example.

Before long, buried problems are excavated and participants bring their real feelings into the open. Long-neglected issues that no one was prepared to confront before because they implied criticism of people in the room now surface and are resolved. Everyone leaves the retreat with a feeling of accomplishment and with stronger bonds to the company and the other executives.

Here, once again, we see an act of empathy—the chairman's willingness to admit a serious mistake—being the launching pad to dialogue. The irony is that the chairman stumbled upon it by accident. He had thought that by dressing casually in slacks and a sweater and by inviting the participants to be frank with him, he was creating the proper conditions for dialogue. He obviously knew that something was needed to make the other executives feel free enough to treat him and each other as equals. But he chose the wrong gesture. In effect, he wasted three quarters of the time available for dialogue before stumbling unintentionally on the right gesture of empathy.

Unfortunately, it is all too common for executives to assume that appearances are what counts. The most autocratic executives think that by inviting others to call them by their first name and dressing casually they can create a climate of equality. We should recall that the philosopher Martin Buber thought that dialogue between people in inherently unequal positions was not possible. Further experience with dialogue has shown that it *is* possible but that it doesn't happen automatically or through making superficial gestures. It was the chairman's obvious sincerity in taking public responsibility for a serious mistake that finally broke the ice, putting participants on a more equal footing and permitting them to open themselves to the risks of dialogue.

In some respects, planning for dialogue in advance is easier to pull off than spontaneous dialogue. This is because there is usually more time to correct missteps, as in the example above, and also because the rules of the game can be explained to people in advance. In spontaneous dialogue, no one makes a formal announcement: "Folks, we are about to begin dialogue, so fasten your seat belts." Dialogue is sometimes so random and elusive that a flash of it can come and go without anyone even noticing it.

But planned dialogue can also be complex because it is still an unfamiliar process; the opportunities for it to go awry are boundless. I have seen planned dialogue ruined by many common mistakes, such as choosing the wrong kind of facilitator, not allocating enough time for the dialogue to do its work, and—the most common of all—cutting off the dialogue prematurely in the interest of achieving closure and reaching a decision.

Some of the most important work in planning business-related dialogues takes place at two related centers at MIT's Sloan School of Management.

Peter Senge is the founder of one of them, the Center for Organizational Learning. Senge and his associates have developed a sophisticated conception of the "learning organization" in which dialogue plays a central role.

One of the examples Senge cites is a two-day dialogue that John MacCarthy, the CEO of the DataQuest company of California, convened with his management team. MacCarthy faced a tough challenge. He had recently followed in the footsteps of the company's founder, a charismatic engineer who over a period of thirty years had carved out a position of leadership for the company in the field of disk drives and computer peripherals. He had done so through a succession of highly creative product innovations.

Throughout the many years of his leadership, the founder had created a corporate culture in which the R-and-D function of the company was regarded as the company's key to success, with marketing, manufacturing, finance, and other business functions playing a supporting role. But the industry had changed. Disk drives were becoming a commodity, competition was fierce, and DataQuest was losing ground.

In his invitation to his associates, MacCarthy was lucid in announcing the purpose of the dialogue he wished to initiate. It was, he stated, solely to "help us to clarify [our] assumptions . . . to gain understanding of each other's view by thinking through the major issues facing us at this time."[1]

Participants hewed to the guidelines, and the dialogue that ensued proved immensely productive. In its earliest stages, the head of marketing was reluctant to state his assumptions frankly, but as the session progressed he gradually opened up. He said he assumed that R and D harbored an image of itself as superior to the other parts of the business. He assumed that R and D saw itself as the "keeper of the flame," responsible for keeping alive the tradition the founder had established and refusing to compromise the creative product innovations on which the company's reputation had been built. He further assumed that R and D would be unresponsive to the full range of customer needs and had little interest in linking the proud DataQuest name with a variety of mundane, pedestrian peripheral products customers wanted or the haggling and hassling that went on in the dealer organization. He also said that in the interest of staying competitive, he had often used his budget to acquire these less creative products because he assumed that R and D would want nothing to do with them.

In response, the head of R and D startled the group with how sharply his own view varied from the buzz within the company. He said he assumed that the split in the company's make/buy decisions (R and D developing the more "creative" products internally, marketing acquiring the more mundane products on the outside) was "just insane" because it prevented an "overriding product strategy" for the company. He added that innovations in manufacturing, marketing, and understanding customer needs were just as creative as the work done by his own group, that he wanted no part of the old "keeper of the flame" tradition because it didn't match either his values or the present situation of the company, and that he was angry at "being saddled with an old stereotype."

The manufacturing VP pointed out that the dominant corporate culture was one of each division holding on to control of its own function rather than letting others in on decisions that affected the whole company and that this culture of control pervaded the relationship between manufacturing and finance as well as that between marketing and R and D.

As the dialogue unfolded, the insights into one another's points of view gained momentum, giving a sense of release to all. Senge reports that this single-session dialogue was so successful that it proved "nothing short of remarkable."[2] It healed a thirty-year rift between marketing and R and D; marketing abandoned its end run around R and D in rounding out the company's product lines; new criteria evolved about the use of the DataQuest name; a new, more empowering and cooperative climate was established; and the corporate culture dropped old stereotypes that were holding the company back. Senge draws lessons from this and other dialogues similar to those I have been advancing.

He agrees that participants must meet as equals. Senge acknowledges the skepticism of thinkers such as Bohm and Buber who suspect that, in hierarchical organizations, dialogue among equals is impossible. But Senge is convinced that it can be done, and my own experience supports his conclusion. Hierarchy is a major obstacle, but it can be overcome if the will and commitment to do so are strong enough.

Senge also stresses that participants have to learn the art of questioning their own assumptions. Most people are habituated to defending their assumptions. But in dialogue, participants must learn how to suspend them. An important aspect of dialogic skill is being willing to entertain the possibility that one's own assumptions might be wrong and those of other participants might be right.[3]

Senge does not claim that all dialogues achieve extraordinary results. But again, based on my own experience, I find his conclusions credible. Admittedly, the DataQuest executives come across as highly intelligent people who entered the dialogue with trust, goodwill, and good faith. But these conditions are hardly unique. As Senge points out, "Deep down there is a longing for dialogue, especially on issues of the utmost importance to us."

Focus Groups

The simplest and most rudimentary form of planned dialogue arises in focus groups of consumers, voters, or workers brought together for a few brief hours. The explicit purpose of focus groups is to conduct research on people's attitudes. It is not to do dialogue or engage in general discussion of issues.

Yet after experience with hundreds of focus groups, I have learned that the most productive ones are those that create dialogue.

Focus groups are generally composed of eight to twelve people convened for about two hours solely for the purpose of reacting to an issue, a candidate, a product, or a communication. Typically, the participants do not know one another; they are usually selected to represent the full diversity of the public. After their brief encounter, most focus group participants will never meet again. They are strangers coming from different social classes, areas, and backgrounds. Yet even under these conditions genuine dialogue can be planned—even on subjects where people are bitterly divided, as, for example, race relations.

Black and white participants are often mixed together in focus groups to discuss such racially sensitive topics as crime, welfare, teenage pregnancy, and affirmative action. Typically, at the start of a two-hour focus group session on a sensitive issue, a polite but distant coldness prevails. Both the black and white participants pick their words carefully. You can almost smell the self-censoring and smoldering tension beneath the polite language. The air is thick with racial self-consciousness and unspoken views.

In discussing affirmative action, for example, most white participants reject racial preferences while most black participants support them. As the conversation unfolds under the guidance of a skilled moderator and participants begin to reveal their assumptions, the reason for the stark contrast grows clear: it is lack of trust on both sides. Whites express the fear that because of affirmative action, less qualified black people will replace better-qualified whites in jobs or at select schools. Blacks are fearful that without affirmative action, less qualified whites will prevent qualified black people from getting the jobs and school choices they deserve.

If sufficient rapport has been established in the group, it gradually dawns on both sides that they share a wide area of agreement. Both believe that merit should be the deciding factor. What really separates them is that they don't trust the other side to be fair in judging merit.

For most participants, this is the first time they have ever attempted to talk openly about so sensitive an issue in an interracial setting. Honest dialogue between black people and white where both sides share their real feelings is largely absent in American public life. Most people shy away from the discomfort of voicing their views to those who disagree with them, particularly when angry and hostile feelings are involved. As a result, outside of focus groups, these views are expressed in private to like-minded people of the same race, where they fester and poison the atmosphere.

When people mistrust each other, lack of dialogue greatly exacerbates the mistrust: when you cannot engage people in serious dialogue, particularly those from a different race or religion, you invariably transform them into a stereotype. You attribute unappealing motivations to them. You distance them from yourself and your own kind. You depersonalize them, preventing bonds of empathy from forming that can serve as a base for building mutual trust and understanding.

The kind of interracial dialogue that occurs in a focus group is not some rare and mystical experience; it is the most ordinary and mundane form of conversation. Yet most of the time the atmosphere in the focus group is transformed by the end of the two hours. This is not to say that black and white participants who start as hostile strangers to each other part as friends. They remain strangers. Nonetheless, something important has transpired between them: a fragile bond of mutual respect has been forged. Each side has been obliged by circumstances to hear the other talk about a concern of common interest in a way that strikes a responsive chord.

In almost every successful focus group, rapport is achieved when someone admits to a concern that others share but are reluctant to express openly. For example, the US organization Public Agenda conducted a focus group on crime in Baltimore that brought together whites and blacks. One could feel the whites react with relief when a black woman pointed out that young black males in her part of town were particularly dangerous and that she avoided certain neighborhoods because she was afraid. She was acknowledging something whites felt but were afraid to mention for fear of seeming racist. After she brought this out, the discussion turned to the media's reporting of race and crime, and the white participants criticized the media's needless emphasis on the color of criminals who had already been caught. These statements helped to create rapport with the black participants.

A similar phenomenon occurs in all successful focus groups, not just those involving race. In a Public Agenda study on primary school education, a focus group included a businessman, teachers, and parents. The businessman raised the issue of teacher tenure; he talked about how accountability worked in the real world and couldn't understand why teachers were protected from it when he and his employees were not. One teacher took him on, and they engaged in a lively but respectful debate that (thanks to the facilitator's subtle guidance) gradually segued into dialogue. By the end of the session, they liked each other and were looking to each other for feedback on their thinking. They still didn't agree with each other, but they had developed respect and sympathy for each other's viewpoints. At one point, the moderator remarked that they seemed like an old married couple, and everyone laughed. When the session ended, they stood in the corridor, continuing the conversation, mindless of the fact that it was already 10 P.M.

A similar pattern unfolds in focus groups of people selected at random to discuss abortion. Here again, the racial factor is not at issue: participants may all be white or all black. But the conversation starts with the same guardedness and self-consciousness. Participants are on the alert for opposition. Almost at all costs, they want to avoid the discomfort of confrontation. All have seen confrontations on television where prolife and prochoice adherents engage each other in bitter, even nasty, disputes. In an average focus group, most participants will go out of their way to avoid this kind of unpleasantness.

As the two-hour session progresses, the early mood of suspicion and reserve gradually dissipates. Participants are surprised to learn that those in the group who disagree with their position (either prolife or prochoice), nonetheless share their concerns. Hardly ever is anyone as dogmatic and self-righteous as the advocates they have seen and heard on television. Typically, in a focus group, some of the prochoice people admit to reservations about their own position and agree that the concerns of the prolife people worry them also, and at least some of the prolife people admit to their own reservations. Here, once again, people's stereotypes of the "other" (whether the other is liberal, conservative, Christian, secular humanist, or dogcatcher) melt away. As these stereotypes dissipate, they are replaced by glimmerings of respect and fragile bonds of community.

In all focus groups, once deeply ingrained stereotypes are broken, people are free to hear what is being said. If they then signal that they have really heard the point of view of the other sympathetically, the atmosphere begins to change. People feel less need to defend their own position, they start to take in the other point of view, and dialogue begins. It reverts back to discussion only at the point when the high energy and concentration needed for dialogue begin to flag.

It is hardly an exaggeration to state that in focus groups where those holding contrary views have been demonized, each side makes the unexpected discovery that the other is human: a kindred soul who laughs at the same jokes and has similar worries. Of course, there may be disagreement on the substance of the issues, particularly on controversial issues such as affirmative action and abortion. But a groundwork of goodwill, mutuality, and identity has been laid that makes further dialogue possible. In a brief period of time, listening empathically, treating one another as equals, and talking openly about assumptions create an opening for mutual understanding that probably cannot be created any other way.

In focus groups, dialogue happens only occasionally, as a by-product of a research process. Dialogue is far more common in citizen forums among those who meet for the purpose of discussing issues of common concern. In 1995, a three-day meeting of Americans selected from a variety of cities took place in Texas. The purpose of the meeting was to test an idea that political scientist James Fishkin had advanced. Fishkin wanted to test his hypothesis that bringing average Americans together to deliberate seriously on a variety of issues would show public opinion in a different light than ordinary public opinion polls reveal. His theory held that once people have an opportunity to deliberate with others, their opinions change.

The test proved inconclusive. There was less substantive

changing of minds after the several days of deliberation than
Fishkin had anticipated.[4] But one unanticipated by-product
of the experiment was abundantly clear: these groups of ran-
domly selected Americans, who had never met one another
before and had little in common, ended the sessions with respect for the points of view of the other participants (as well
as personal warmth and acceptance). It was an encounter
they cherished. Yet their only relationship throughout the
three days was one of talking seriously with one another
about a variety of divisive political issues.

Large numbers of people participate regularly in National
Issues Forums (NIFs) that meet in schools, libraries, churches,
civic organizations, and even prisons all over the US. For almost twenty years, two organizations with which I am affiliated, the Kettering Foundation and Public Agenda, have
helped to expedite these forums and have prepared special
"issues books" so that participants can consider concrete
choices for each issue the forums address. Over the past few
years, these citizen groups have treated issues such as health
care, crime, public education, Social Security, and environ-
mental protection. The forums create an atmosphere in which
status and power differences are minimized, people can truly
listen to one another, and opportunities are created to make
assumptions explicit.

For the past several years, Public Agenda has been conven-
ing citizens and educators to talk about how to improve the
quality of public education in America. In collaboration with
the Institute for Educational Leadership, Public Agenda has
introduced a process, called "Public Conversations About the
Public's Schools," that is designed to help community members sort out their differences and find common ground on
how to improve local schools.

The Public Conversations meetings employ a "choice-work" approach in which issues such as school standards, vouchers, and funding are framed in the form of concrete choices and formulated in the language of average citizens, not in professional jargon. They focus on the kinds of concerns and values that nonexperts can readily address.

Three out of four people who attend these meetings report that they improve their understanding of educational issues better than meetings with experts or politicians. They also report encountering points of view different from their own that cause them to see the problems of the schools in a new light.

One such meeting took place in a rural US school district. Twenty participants of diverse backgrounds had been invited to talk about parental involvement while a number of school board members and district staff observed.

Just before the meeting, a man who was not on the invitation list joined the group. He had failed in a run for school board and was well known as a difficult character who had raised a significant amount of hell at past public meetings.

Rather than the impending disaster it had at first seemed, his presence made the dynamics of the meeting all the more convincing. For while the group was diverse (school parents, a home schooler, a minister, a business leader, two or three teachers, a community college person, a principal, a school counselor, and so on), most of the members knew and were comfortable with one another. The new arrival was the exception. After he took a couple of early shots at the district and teachers, he seemed to adjust to the setting of the meeting, finding the discussion materials fair and useful and accepting the spirit and norms of the group. He began waiting his turn to talk and became more and more constructive as the conversation went on. At the end of the evening, he shook hands with the superintendent and thanked her for letting him participate. She and the board members who were present later expressed amazement at how he had reacted to the proceedings.

An even more successful meeting took place in Maine, in the midst of a flood that closed roads and shut down the entire water supply to nearby Portland. Despite these hardships, approximately seventy of the expected ninety members of the community managed to attend. And despite a past history of extreme acrimony, particularly about school budget battles, the dialogue format was so successful that the moderators formed themselves into a local public service organization called Seeking Public Agreement for Next Steps (SPANS). Since the initial town meeting, SPANS has been called on by the community to facilitate public conversation on a number of other issues, and recently, after numerous failures, SPANS helped get a school budget passed in an atmosphere of unheard-of harmony.

These citizen meetings typically give rise to flashes of dialogue where people engage one another so honestly and directly that one can almost see the bonds of community form before one's eyes. The dialogues in the focus groups and citizen forums illustrate strategies we have encountered in earlier examples.

Finding the Common Interest

In their dialogue on affirmative action, the white and black participants started by emphasizing the divisive interests that separated them: whites bitterly opposing affirmative action, black people strongly supporting it. Gradually, however, the focus shifted to a vital interest both groups shared in common: the belief that fairness should prevail. Once the dialogue moved toward this shared value, the gap between the two groups narrowed and the conversation focused on how to ensure fairness of results. An ideological confrontation was thus channeled into a practical consideration of tactics.

Gestures of Empathy

In the abortion focus group, participants were relieved—and surprised—to learn that those who held views contrary to their own nonetheless shared many of their own concerns. This mutual acknowledgment of the legitimacy of the point of view of the other is the kind of gesture of respect and empathy that almost always helps to transform mundane discussion into dialogue.

Transforming Transactions into Relationships

The focus group dialogues illustrate that disagreement on the substance of issues need not lead to mutual hostility. On emotion-laden issues such as abortion and race relations, much of the hostility that people ordinarily feel toward those who hold views contrary to their own grows out of stereotyping the views of one's opponent. Dialogue encourages participants to cut through such stereotypes and instead encounter flesh-and-blood people.

Often, to their own surprise, participants discover affinities with people with whom they strongly disagree. This experience transforms a battle between distorting stereotypes into a human encounter between people who feel a bond with one another even though their life experience has led them in different directions.

STRATEGY

Where applicable, identify mistrust as the real source of misunderstandings.

There is no greater obstacle to dialogue than mistrust. This reality became evident once we turned from spontaneous to planned dialogue. It was not obvious in spontaneous dialogue for the simple reason that when mistrust is present, no spontaneous dialogue will arise.

The moment we turn to planned dialogue, however, we realize that a minimum level of trust must exist for dialogue to proceed. If it does not exist, conversation remains at the level of discussion. It can shift to dialogue if something happens, such as a gesture of empathy that helps to dissipate the mistrust or at least to bring it into the open. We saw this happen in a number of the dialogues in this chapter, particularly in the focus group on race and the chemical company retreat.

In each instance, participants realized that mistrust was causing them to hold back. In these examples, the mistrust was relatively easy to deal with. In the next chapter we will encounter more difficult forms of planned dialogue with deeper levels of mistrust. If the mistrust is not deep or personal, a reasonably straightforward strategy is simply to bring it to the surface. To do this, either you can offer a gestire of empathy that addresses the mistrust or you can say something like "I know that we may not fully trust each other, but let's try to talk things out for the sake of our common objective, or at least so that we can understand each other better."

STRATEGY

Err on the side of including people who disagree.

When US President Bill Clinton established a special committee to launch a year of national dialogue on race in 1997, he was severely—and rightly—criticized for including only like-minded people. For example, he excluded all critics of affirmative action. The initial meetings of the committee therefore took the form of preaching to the converted rather than genuine dialogue. Realizing his error, the president invited several well-known opponents of affirmative action for dialogue at the White House, with results that left everyone feeling much better about the process. In these dialogues, the opponents of affirmative action left feeling that they had been heard in a respectful and honorable fashion. Some of the mistrust between the two sides was dissipated when those holding opposing views acknowledged the good faith of the other side, rather than dismissing their views contemptuously.

Something of the same sort took place in the Nevada school district. The first impulse of the participants, understandably, was to exclude the man who had previously been disruptive and was known to be in disagreement with the majority. His presence turned out, however, to contribute to the authenticity and richness of the dialogue that ensued.

A majority of the meetings I am obliged to attend come closer to the preaching-to-the-converted model than to dialogue. This is because it is much easier to spend time congratulating people who agree with you on the wisdom of their views than to seek mutual understanding with people holding different views. But dialogue requires seeking out a variety of points of view, rather than merely reinforcing one's own preexisting beliefs. Our society possesses an abundance of rituals for morale-boosting; it possesses precious few for gaining the mutual understanding that comes from dialogue.

STRATEGY

Encourage relationships in order to humanize transactions.

I need not dwell on this strategy since I have already discussed it. But it must be included in the inventory because it is indispensable to dialogue. Reaching out to others during transactions to develop relationships, however brief or casual, is a strategy that most people follow automatically and intuitively. For example, it is almost instinctive for people who have been meeting to have lunch or dinner together even if it serves no practical purpose. All of us are drawn to the ancient ritual of breaking bread together.

Other cultures often understand this symbolism better than we do in our eagerness to conduct business even during meals. But deep down, all of us realize that communication with one another is not confined to the level of impersonal transactions; on the contrary, the most profound forms of communication take place at the deeper level of personal encounter—the level of I-Thou relationships. Given the slightest chance, people gravitate in this direction.

STRATEGY

Expose old scripts to a reality check.

Each of us sees reality from our own highly conditioned perspective—the web of beliefs, values, assumptions, and customs that have shaped our views over decades of experience. We interpret events according to our own unwritten "scripts." These scripts are formed partially through individual experience and partially through the experience of organizations. Well-established institutions develop a potent corporate culture that envelops people as soon as they become part of the institution.

Sometimes these corporate cultures grow obsolete; their rituals and value systems persist even when circumstances have changed beyond recognition. Then people find themselves caught up in practices that no longer make sense and may even be dysfunctional. Clearly, this was going on in the DataQuest dialogue. The dialogue served as a valuable reality check. As soon as the participants brought their assumptions into the open, it became clear that each was interpreting the behavior and motives of the others according to the script written in the time of the founder, a script that was no longer relevant to today's realities. Because the participants were able to draw upon a heritage of goodwill and collegiality, they were quick to edit the script appropriately. Dialogue is an excellent way of editing obsolete scripts.

Let us now turn to examples of planned dialogues that present far greater obstacles to mutual understanding than those we have encountered thus far.

Chapter 7

The Long and the Short of It

William Isaacs, who heads the Dialogue Center at MIT's Sloan School of Management, describes a dialogue between organized labor and management in a large steel mill. At the time of the dialogue, conditions in the mill were desperate. Under competitive pressure from more efficient minimills, the company had downsized from 5,000 employees to fewer than 1,000. The dialogue was part of a program to help the mill survive in the new competitive environment. The problem was that despite the threat to their mutual survival, management and labor were barely able to talk to each other with civility.

When the dialogue began, it quickly became apparent that years of adversarial relations had created an almost unbridgeable heritage of bitterness and bad blood between union and management. The climate was much too divisive for the sort of ordinary dialogue that can be conducted on a weekend retreat, as in the chemical company and the computer disk company. There was not enough trust and goodwill to establish the minimum trust needed for dialogue, despite the recognition on both sides that the future of the company was at stake. Under Isaacs's guidance, the meetings between the two adversaries took place over a period of many months in a long series of sessions. In the early sessions, the mistrust was so intense that participants from both the union and the management side called each other insulting names, stormed out of meetings, and even threw chairs at each other.

Eventually some ground rules were agreed upon. Participants would meet every two weeks, sitting in a circle, without an agenda or specific task or timetable. From the outset, the company president, who participated in all the sessions, displayed an openness of mind and an attitude of equality toward both his fellow executives and the union's representatives. "None of us has *the* answer," he insisted, "but together we might find a *better* answer."

In the early sessions, old habits prevailed. The union participants stuck to the party line, being careful never to disagree with one another in front of management. The party line was that whatever problems occurred in the plant were always management's fault. As the union president said later on, "When we first started, the only thing we ever talked about was the past: how you screwed me in the past, how you lied to me in the past . . . how you promised job security."

For a long time, sessions were tension-ridden, generating hostility and feelings of instability. Old bargaining patterns asserted themselves. As one manager observed, the group would automatically slide into negotiations ("We want this and this." "Well, if we give you this, you have got to give us that."). At times everyone felt frustrated and defensive, finding themselves defending positions even in the face of evidence that they were wrong. The lack of a familiar structure left the group disoriented and without a clear sense of where it was heading—a situation in which polarization easily arises.

In this climate of anxiety, mistrust, and lack of structure, a facilitator (Isaacs) was indispensable. Isaacs, who performed more like a referee than a facilitator, reassured the participants that tension and instability were a normal part of the process. And he kept reiterating the ground rules: the participants should not panic, walk out, or choose to fight or "kiss off" someone else's point of view. Instead, they should simply *listen,* not only to what others were saying but also to what they themselves were saying.

Gradually the tone shifted. Both sides stopped blaming the other. The steelworkers started to recognize that they had more in common with management than they had initially assumed. All of the participants became less dogmatic. They started to bring their assumptions into the open and to test them against experience.

They came to realize that no single point of view seemed totally correct but that each helped to fit the pieces of the puzzle together. The old adversarial attitude slowly dissipated. As one trade union member said with a sense of wonderment, "You know, I can't tell who is on what side anymore." Another observed about his own responses, "I used to need to attack. Now, if someone says something I don't agree with, so what?" A manager observed, "We created a space to listen to each other . . . so that people can learn the values of *various* people as opposed to the *same* people."

Clearly, this type of dialogue among groups that deeply mistrust each other requires its own special strategy. The following strategy is therefore an important one.

STRATEGY

Minimize the level of mistrust before pursuing practical objectives.

A moment's reflection on the core conditions of dialogue shows that mistrust must inevitably inhibit dialogue. It is difficult to empathize with people you mistrust and to treat them as a "Thou." And you may feel too vulnerable to reveal your deepest assumptions in the presence of those you mistrust.

At the same time, however, dialogue is a trust-building process. How, then, can you establish the minimum level of trust needed to start a dialogue and then gradually build up enough to pursue a common objective?

The appropriate tactics for doing so vary according to the severity of the mistrust problem. In earlier examples of dialogue, simple acts of empathy were enough to break through a thin crust of mistrust so as to permit dialogue to unfold. In the example of the focus group with equal numbers of white and black participants, the dialogue was able to proceed despite deeper levels of mistrust because its goal was confined to gaining mutual understanding; it did not require the group to arrive at practical decisions. If, instead of a focus group, it had been an official commission required to make practical recommendations for action, a great deal more effort would have been needed to reduce the level of mistrust.

In the steel mill example, the layers of mistrust built up over decades blocked the participants from pursuing their objective of working together to compete and survive in a changed marketplace. Inching the participants toward dialogue under these circumstances required Isaacs to resort to a variety of tactics going far beyond individual acts of empathy. He was obliged to serve as referee, to abandon a specific agenda, to throw away a timetable limiting the number of sessions, and to insist on only one inviolable rule: that participants hang in and simply *listen*—to themselves as well as to everyone else.

Eventually the process worked and the conditions were transformed from those of an armed camp to a team who worked together well enough to turn defeat into victory.

Let us turn now to the work of a man who routinely conducts dialogue under even worse conditions of mistrust than those in the steel mill. Harold Saunders is a former diplomat and public servant and is presently affiliated with the Kettering Foundation. For many years, Saunders has been practicing dialogue among groups of people who come from different cultures, who profoundly mistrust one another, and who have a long history of mutual enmity.

I first encountered Harold Saunders in the early 1980s, when, with a Soviet counterpart, he was attempting to find common ground on which the United States and the Soviet Union could forge agreement on a variety of regional conflicts in the Middle East, Africa, Central America, and especially Afghanistan. Having flown on the Henry Kissinger shuttles and worked at Camp David with Jimmy Carter, Menachem Begin, and Anwar Sadat as a government official in the 1970s, in the 1980s Saunders turned to nonofficial dialogue with Arabs and Israelis in the interest of advancing the peace process. For many years now, Saunders has been facilitating dialogue with people who could hardly be further apart from each other in their emotions and their frameworks of assumptions.

Before he discovered the great power of dialogue, Saunders had come to recognize the limits of traditional diplomacy. He disliked the gamesmanship of diplomatic negotiation at its most contentious, where participants spend much of their time making "points" at one another's expense. He became convinced that these sorts of negotiations were worse than a waste of time, especially when they took place between rivals such as the Soviet Union and the United States in the throes of the Cold War. "All that traditional diplomacy of this sort does," he says, "is to dig people further into their rigid, set positions. If they misunderstood each other to start with, you can be sure that traditional diplomacy at its worst will deepen the misunderstanding." In this sense, diplomacy can be likened to introducing lawyers into a divorce proceeding. For legal reasons you may need the lawyers, but you can almost guarantee that the parties will grow more hostile to each other once lawyers get involved.

Saunders is high in his praise of artful diplomats and does not reject hard negotiating to resolve conflicting interests. But he sees a need for dialogue to *precede* such negotiations, just as it should precede decision making on sensitive issues in organizations.

Saunders argues that in dialogue, old enemies can learn to break through stereotypes and come to see each other as whole human beings like themselves, with points of view that make sense if seen from their own perspective. Without such dialogue, he believes, the chances of successful negotiations are greatly reduced, even when rational self-interest might argue for success. When passions and ideologies are involved and cultures clash, rational self-interest can quickly recede into the background. It takes the more arduous forms of dialogue to let passions cool enough for negotiable self-interest to come to the fore. And like the growth of a seedling, developing mutual respect takes time—often a great deal of it.

When the Cold War ended and the Soviet Union dissolved, Saunders and his Russian colleague decided to formalize the process of sustained dialogue they had learned in more than twenty semiannual Soviet-U.S. meetings throughout the 1980s. They describe it as a progression of five stages:

- First, a third party carefully selects about a dozen participants reflecting the views of the main factions in the conflict.
- Second, in the first few meetings, they ventilate their problems and grievances and analyze their relationship. Eventually, they identify one problem above all others that they need to work on first.
- Third, they affirm their definition of the problem, lay out choices for dealing with it, weigh those choices, and begin to develop a sense of direction for dealing with the problem they have identified.
- Fourth, they reflect on the obstacles they are likely to encounter, what steps will overcome those obstacles, who can take those steps, and how they can be arranged as a plan of action in the larger body politic.
- Fifth, if they feel conditions permit, they advance beyond dialogue to discuss what action they can take themselves or how to place the plan of action in the hands of those who have the capacity to act.

In describing these stages, Saunders implies no rigidity of sequence. Participants move back and forth across stages as they cope with new situations or rethink earlier assumptions. In a prolonged dialogue, each session may see them circling back to stage three as they tackle a new problem to deal with events that have taken place since the previous session. In his tactics, Saunders differs somewhat from Isaacs, but both have adapted their techniques to pursue the strategy cited above, namely, minimizing the level of mistrust through dialogue before pursuing practical objectives.

Saunders and his Russian colleague decided to apply this process to one of the conflicts that had broken out on the territory of the former Soviet Union. They chose Tajikistan, the poorest of the former Soviet republics, located on the southern Soviet border with Afghanistan. Independence had been thrust on this republic, which had never before known existence as an independent state, and in 1992 it had slipped quickly into a vicious civil war in which more than 50,000 people (out of a population of 5 million) had died and perhaps as many as 700,000 had been driven from their homes.

In March 1993, a group of about a dozen influential Tajikistanis with roots in different regions, nationalities, and political movements within the civil war sat down together for the first time. Subsequently, they held at least twenty meetings and are still going strong. Saunders characterizes them as having become "a mind at work in the middle of a country making itself." In contrast to a task force, which works on an assigned problem and then disbands, this group learned to talk, think, and work together in new ways that made them almost a microcosm of what a unified Tajikistan might look like.

When they sat down together for the first time, the participants could barely look at one another, so pained and angry were they with one another. During their initial three-day sessions, they spent most of their time grieving for their tragically divided country. On a hot August afternoon on the third day of their meeting in an old Russian convent, one of the participants observed, "What we really have to work on is starting negotiations between the government and the opposition on creating conditions for the return of the refugees. Nothing else in our country can happen until that happens."

While they could take the problem no further in that meeting, they came together two months later and had their first real dialogue on how to deal cooperatively with the problem they had defined together. How could a negotiation be put together? The opposition was geographically dispersed over several countries and covered an ideological spectrum from militant Muslims to moderate democrats. How could a group like that come to the table? "Who will come?" asked participants. "What about people responsible for killing? Will they be invited?"

Between that meeting and the next, representatives of opposition elements met in Iran and drafted a common platform. In later dialogue sessions, each side made explicit its assumptions about why it feared the others, and in their sixth session they wrote their first joint memorandum, "Memorandum on a Negotiating Process for Tajikistan." In a little more than a year, they had moved from a group whose members could barely talk with one another to a group that could write a joint memorandum on a negotiating process that could become the core of a political process of national reconciliation in their country. When the official negotiating team sat down, three of the delegates were participants in the dialogue.

While the official negotiations were under way, participants in the dialogue said, "What we have to work on now is designing a political process of national reconciliation in Tajikistan," which they proceeded to do. The dialogue is still going on. A series of peace agreements was formalized in the presence of Russian president Boris Yeltsin at the end of June 1997, and the participants in the dialogue then turned their attention to the "postaccord phase." Their attention has now shifted to how they can replicate their kind of dialogue in key places throughout Tajikistan as its people try to turn a formal peace agreement into a peaceful country. They have published their joint memoranda as encouragement to others. In the first four years of this prolonged dialogue, the participants developed a mutual respect and liking for one another without giving up any element of their own ethnic identity or religious beliefs.[1]

THE ISSUE OF LENGTH

From the many varieties of dialogue I have reviewed, it is clear that the rules for conducting them vary—sometimes enormously—depending on the situation or on such factors as the level of mistrust. One of the most difficult skills to acquire in doing dialogue is the ability to become aware of how to adjust the format of a dialogue to fit various conditions.

Dialogue formats will vary according to how ambitious the goals of the dialogue group are. Some practitioners of dialogue such as Harold Saunders have very ambitious goals, such as helping to make peace among old adversaries: Arabs and Israelis, Serbs and Croats, pro- and antiabortion advocates. Other advocates of dialogue (myself included) usually have less ambitious goals, such as bringing together people from different subcultures (e.g., business, science, academia, political leaders, community organizations) to find common ground in the interest of advancing a shared objective.

The scope of one's objectives dictates the practical dimensions of dialogue, especially its duration. Dialogue that must bridge an enormous gap of mistrust and cultural misunderstanding (for example, the gap separating French- and English-speaking Canadians on the subject of national unity) may go on for years. Dialogue among groups who simply bring different assumptions to the table without a heavy baggage of mistrust may take only one or two sessions. Choosing the right length for dialogue requires making a number of practical decisions:

- How many sessions will there be?
- With what frequency will they be held?
- What kinds of people should participate?
- Should they be helped by professional facilitators or not?
- What will the setting be?
- With what expectations should the participants come to the table?

If these questions are not answered in advance, they can generate a great deal of bewilderment. It is not necessary to have precise answers to all of them, but there should be some rules of thumb that can guide the dialogue planning.

DIALOGUE AS A CONTINUUM

It is useful to think of dialogue as a continuum ranging from spontaneous dialogues that last only a few minutes to formal dialogues that are planned in advance and unfold over weeks, months, or even years, and where meticulous attention is given to the setting, composition, and agenda of the group. Dialogue among long-standing opponents separated by culture, mistrust, and conflicting interests may require all manner of formal arrangements and run on for an indefinite period of time. It is interesting to note, however, that even the two extremes of the spectrum—the brief, spontaneous moment of dialogue between friends or colleagues and the full-court multiple-year dialogue between enemies—must meet the core conditions of empathic listening, equality of standing, and the laying bare of assumptions for the purpose of deepening insight and understanding and preparing the ground for decision making.

A lengthier, more extended dialogue requires considerable training and discipline and may stir participants to the depths of their being. This kind of dialogue is indicated when a great emotional and cognitive distance needs to be traversed and the journey to mutual understanding is beset with obstacles. So profound can the effects of such a dialogue be in calling into question people's most cherished assumptions that they sometimes leave participants disoriented and bewildered, as well as transformed in positive ways.[2]

The single greatest variation in dialogue is length. Brief dialogues planned in advance typically require one to three sessions, ideally in informal settings with one or several meals taken together if possible. If a trained person facilitates the dialogue, he or she must—unless an impasse is reached or the ground rules are flagrantly violated—get out of the way once the purpose of the dialogue is enunciated, a provocative question is raised, and guidelines are established.

For extended dialogue, on the other hand, success depends on whether one is prepared to make a major commitment of multiple sessions conducted regularly (even on a weekly basis), extending from six months to several years. Exquisite care must go into planning these kinds of dialogues; a skilled facilitator is probably essential at the beginning (although she should expect to work herself out of a job once the group settles into its work). While the ultimate purpose of the dialogue must be clear to all participants, it is not wise to impose a strict or narrow agenda on the group.

For those planning dialogues, the most important practical

decision is what the length of the dialogue should be. This decision is an important one. If one chooses wrongly, the result will be either failure by overkill, with the participants losing patience, or failure by underestimating the amount of dialogic work that needs to be done, with participants ending up frustrated, turned off, or angry.

There are several techniques for making this important decision. Perhaps the most important is focusing on how a dialogue's format relates to its purpose. Once one knows the specific purpose of a dialogue, it should be possible to place it toward one end of the spectrum or the other. For example, my usual purpose in doing dialogue is to bring together people on policy issues that do not require surmounting a heritage of mistrust or irreconcilable conflicts of interest. These kinds of dialogue fall at the brief rather than the extended end of the dialogue spectrum.

If any one of the following four criteria applies, the dialogue automatically belongs in the extended dialogue category (i.e., requiring a commitment of at least six months' duration with frequent meetings):

1. A deep and prolonged heritage of mistrust has kept the participants apart.
2. A serious conflict of interest of religious-type intensity divides the participants.
3. The participants must abandon their familiar and comfortable conceptual frameworks and paradigms for new ways of thinking and knowing.
4. The purpose is to move the participants to deeper levels of intimacy or to higher levels of thought than any one individual may be capable of achieving.

Conversely, dialogue will automatically fall at the brief end of the spectrum (that is, a minimal commitment to no more than two or three several-hour sessions) if it meets these criteria:

1. The participants trust each other or at least have no reason for mistrust.
2. Conflicts of interest are readily bridged.
3. The participants share the same culture, subculture, and language.
4. The ambition of the dialogue is limited to reaching mutual understanding on a specific, easily defined issue.

There are many instances where the decision about length cannot be made automatically and the time commitment will fall between the two extremes. Dialogues in the middle range of the spectrum will generally require less than six months but more than one or two sessions—for example, a series of four or five meetings, some of which may extend overnight or to entire weekends. These more ambiguous situations tend to arise when participants trust one another, speak the same language, and share the same culture but bring with them widely disparate frameworks of assumptions or come from different subcultures; for example, businesspeople and academics, journalists and teachers, and managers from a variety of companies, disciplines, and industries.

The accompanying list shows a wide range of dialogue purposes. Some call for extended dialogue, some for brief dialogue, and some fall in the middle range. The relationship between purpose and length is not always clear in advance, but for most purposes a high degree of correlation exists.

THE LINK BETWEEN PURPOSE AND LENGTH

Brief dialogue when . . .

1. Examining issues from various points of view.
2. Achieving mutual understanding prior to decision making.
3. Bringing together people with shared interests who trust each other.
4. Getting leaders and followers to understand each other's position on a specific issue.
5. Enhancing mutual understanding among groups in a community on a specific issue.

Midrange dialogue when . . .

6. Working through an emotion-driven issue.
7. Reaching across the chasm of gender differences.
8. Reaching across the chasm of subculture differences.
9. Achieving teamwork within the same organization.
10. Preparing the ground for decision making on a sensitive issue.

Midrange or extended dialogue when . . .

11. Seeking common ground among people who hold opposing views on controversial issues such as affirmative action, abortion, and immigration.

Extended dialogue when . . .

12. Preparing the ground for negotiations between opponents who mistrust one another and who come from different cultures.
13. Achieving higher levels of teamwork among organizations with different subcultures.
14. Working together to develop a new paradigm.
15. Tapping into people's pooled experience in the interest of achieving a higher level of thought and intimacy.

A FATAL FORMAT MISTAKE

Length is not the only format decision one needs to make. Other format decisions (for example, whether or not to use a facilitator and, if so, what kind) can also determine the success or failure of the dialogue.

Here is an example of how this kind of format mistake undermined an otherwise well-conceived dialogue. The convenors of the dialogue, a consortium of foundations in the US, had gone to great trouble and expense to bring together a well-selected group of artists and performers mixed with foundation executives committed to funding the arts. Their purpose was one that dialogue is ideally equipped to meet: enhancing mutual understanding among people with shared interests who face a common threat—in this instance, drastic reductions in federal support for the arts. The setting, an old plantation in the US South, though inconvenient to get to, was gracious and warm, creating an ambience conducive to dialogue.

The format mistake grew out of a constraint common to most dialogues: not enough time. Serious dialogue among a fairly large group of strangers requires time for all of them to settle down and get beyond the inevitable showboating and plumage displays to an honest expression of feelings, fears, assumptions, and convictions. Insufficient time is a familiar problem, and there are many ways of working around it. In this instance, the convenors chose the wrong way.

They had secured the services of a professional facilitator and instructed her to make sure that everyone had an equal opportunity to participate. The facilitator implemented these instructions with a heavy hand. She proved to have a perverse genius for cutting off incipient dialogue as soon as it began to emerge, in order, as in a kindergarten, to make sure that those who had remained silent (perhaps because they wanted to listen to or reflect on what was being said) were called upon to take their turn at participating. Ironically, every time dialogue threatened to break out, she succeeded in preventing it from doing so.

The convenors' rationale was understandable: there were lots of prima donnas attending the session, and the convenors, aware of the importance of creating a climate of equality, wanted to make sure that everyone had an equal chance of being heard. The big format mistake the convenors made was inappropriate management of time, reflecting a misguided sense of priorities and a misinterpretation of what equality among participants really means.

Equality in dialogue means that status differences and coercive influences are suspended so that participants can weigh one another's points of view on their intrinsic merits rather than on the authority, power, or prestige of the speaker. It emphatically does not mean apportioning equal quantities of speaking time into neat, orderly packages.

The facilitator imposed a structure for ensuring equal time for all and an orderly sequence of participation. But rigid structure is the enemy of dialogue; it is, as it were, an *antifacilitator*. For the funders and artists to understand each other and to learn to forge a common framework and language, each side needed the time to discover its own assumptions as well as those of other participants. This time-eating process became impossible in a setting where order was imposed and each participant was cut off after a few minutes so that everyone might have his or her brief moment in the sun.

In many settings—and this was one—the term "dialogue facilitator" can prove to be an oxymoron. In this example, the dialogue would have worked much better if the facilitator's task had been defined differently. In most dialogues, facilitators should be heroically unobtrusive and passive. Facilitators are prone to be much too activist: they feel they must earn their fee through constant activity, such as making long lists of the points participants raise and imposing a rigid structure and discipline on the dialogue group.

Tight structure might be appropriate to decision making, but while dialogue may prepare the ground for later decision making, we have seen that the two functions must be kept strictly compartmentalized. A more tuned-in facilitator would simply have acted as a passive traffic cop, not interfering with the traffic as long as it continued to flow.

Summary

Here, for convenience, is a list of the strategies I have been abstracting from the specimens of successful dialogues. They are ordered in a more convenient sequence from that in which I first named them:

Strategy 1: Err on the side of including people who disagree.

Strategy 2: Initiate dialogue through a gesture of empathy.

Strategy 3: Check for the presence of all three core requirements of dialogue—equality, emphatic listening, and surfacing assumptions nonjudgmentally—and learn how to introduce the missing ones.

Strategy 4: Minimize the level of mistrust before pursuing practical objectives.

Strategy 5: Keep dialogue and decision making compartmentalized.

Strategy 6: Focus on common interests, not divisive ones.

Strategy 7: Use specific cases to raise general issues.

Strategy 8: Bring forth your own assumptions before speculating on those of others.

Strategy 9: Clarify assumptions that lead to subculture distortions.

Strategy 10: Where applicable, identify mistrust as the real source of misunderstandings.

Strategy 11: Expose old scripts to a reality check.

Strategy 12: Focus on conflicts between value systems, not people.

Strategy 13: Be sure trust exists before addressing transference distortions.

Strategy 14: When appropriate, express the emotions that accompany strongly held values.

Strategy 15: Encourage relationships in order to humanize transactions.

Although fifteen strategies may seem a large number to keep in mind, in practice most of them become self-evident once they are pointed out (e.g., the strategy of stating your own assumptions before speculating on those of others). There are only a few strategies that require a special effort to remember at all times. For example, during a heated argument, offering a gesture of empathy is not always easy to do. If you are eager to reach closure, it may take great self-discipline to keep dialogue and decision making separate. And it will take practice to learn how to cope with mistrust and how to clarify subtle and well-hidden assumptions.

Chapter 8

Ten Potholes of the Mind

Most dialogue participants will have less difficulty mastering the strategies summarized in the last chapter than overcoming certain deeply ingrained habits that undermine dialogue. So strong are these habits that some people will never do dialogue well. Their personalities are not suited to it. They may be too self-important to respond to others as equals. Or they may not be able to see life from any point of view except their own. They get so locked into their own frameworks that they can't step outside of them. Anyone who has ever argued with a committed Marxist has experienced the frustration of banging one's head against a rigid barrier of thought. The same is true of certain religious fundamentalists, passionate free-market advocates, ideologically committed liberals, and so on.

But such people are in the minority. Most of us, while not wholly exempt from these tendencies, are more flexible and responsive to circumstances. I know many people who get defensive and stop listening when others disagree with them because they feel they are being attacked personally. But once they see that the disagreement is directed at issues rather than at them personally, they drop their defensiveness.

TEN POTHOLES

As a dialogue participant, you may not always be able to avoid the potholes that make the road to dialogue difficult to travel. But you can learn to get through them—*if* you see them in time and learn how to cushion their impact. I have come to think of them as "potholes of the mind," since they arise out of struggles to use one's mind to cope with the challenges of dialogue.

1. Holding Back

The most common complaint among those who conduct dialogue is that, at least in the early stages, some people are reluctant to participate; they hold back, unwilling to commit themselves. When I ask people why they are not more forthcoming, they say something like "Well, you have to be comfortable enough to speak" or "I just wanted to see the way it developed before I got involved." By and large, men are more likely to hold back than women, but often a sense of reserve can pervade the dialogue and affect women as well as men.

The reasons people hold back are varied; the common denominator is that trust has not been built. Because dialogue is so open, a certain amount of self-exposure is involved in it. People hold back whenever they feel any latent hostility in the group or sense the potential for embarrassment. But even when there is no hint of disapproval, they still hold back out of a general wariness so pervasive that I sometimes suspect it is biologically grounded. Most animals are territorial, at home on their own turf and wary outside of it until they get the lay of the land. Doing so takes time and considerable sniffing about.

This pothole is particularly serious for the briefer form of planned dialogue. I recently heard someone growl, "Our dialogue started at ten in the morning and was scheduled to go until four in the afternoon. At about ten minutes to four, someone really opened up and the dialogue began. But by then it was too late."

Suggestion: Professional moderators have learned a number of techniques for breaking the ice and making people feel comfortable enough to plunge into dialogue. Some involve playing games or doing exercises. The approach I like best is to go around the room and ask each participant to say something about his or her own personal past experience that bears on the topic of the dialogue.

On most deeply felt subjects (such as abortion, education reform, capital punishment, or health care), people find it easy to relate the way they feel to a personal experience or memory. Eliciting this experience encourages people to move directly into the subject of the dialogue in a manner that is comfortable for them because they are talking about their own lives and experiences. At the same time, they do not want to risk becoming too personal too quickly among strangers. In dialogue, people learn that they can use their experience without spilling their guts. For example, women who have had an abortion find that they can share their assumptions with others without adopting a confessional tone.

2. Being Locked into a Box

I recall a meeting I attended between business leaders and school heads. Both groups shared an interest in building confidence in schools by enhancing mutual understanding among the key players. But the meeting did not go well. Early in the session, one business leader, the parent of two school students, observed that he and others in his city were disgusted with the seeming inability of the schools to maintain order, particularly the apparent refusal of the schools to deal with troublemakers.

Why, he asked in frustration, is it so difficult to get rid of a chronically disruptive student who is undermining the efforts of the other students to learn? One of the heads reacted politely but pointedly. "In business, if you have a faulty part," he said, "you can throw it away. But you can't throw away a faulty kid and put him out on the streets." He then went on to describe all of the futile efforts his school system had made to deal with disruptive students, but without finding a satisfactory solution. The discussion dragged on with both sides feeling vaguely discontented and misunderstood.

Later, while chatting with the headteacher, I asked him if he had ever considered inviting the business community in his city to organize an off-site facility to mentor and train disruptive students who might respond better to an environment where they could acquire useful work skills.

For a long time he stared at me silently. Then he said quietly that he and his associates rarely reached outside the education world for solutions. "We are tireless," he said, "in ransacking our own system for answers. But we don't look outside for solutions. I'm not saying it's a bad idea or an impractical one. I'm just saying it is something we never do."

For this head, the framework of his thinking was almost literally a box bounded within the world of education. If solutions can be found within the box, however difficult or costly they may be, they will be considered. If solutions lie outside the box, however simple or efficient they may be, they will not be considered. He was clearly uncomfortable with the artificial boundaries of the box, and I admired him for being willing to acknowledge its arbitrariness. Most people are not aware of the boxes that proscribe their thinking and action.

Suggestion: My conversation with the school official happened to occur outside of the formal meeting, but it could—and would—have occurred within it if the meeting had been planned as a dialogue rather than a discussion. In a dialogue, the participants would have devoted a great deal of attention to bringing their assumptions out into the open. In such a context, the superintendent—a dedicated person who was eager to find solutions—would have brought out his assumption, widely shared by education professionals, that the search for solutions is to be restricted to their own world. Had he done so, others would have responded in kind, giving impetus to the dialogic search for deeper insight and understanding. We may not always be able to avoid the potholes that the limits of our experience create, but we can minimize their consequences.

3. Prematurely Moving to Action

Another frequently encountered pothole is a tendency, distinctively American, to rush into action. In a typical discussion, almost as soon as a problem surfaces, someone is bound to say, "Well, what are we going to do about it?" End of dialogue about problem; beginning of a rush of ideas for leaping into the fray and doing something, almost anything, as long as it smacks of taking action rather than more sitting around and talking.

This cultural tendency, a readiness to act on problems, is one of US society's great strengths as well as a limitation. Even a short stay in cultures such as those of England, France, or Russia makes it apparent that Americans typically possess the optimism, energy, and will to confront problems and attempt to solve them.

A focus on swift action, however, gets in the way of doing dialogue. It short-circuits the process of probing the depths of other participants' thoughts, perceptions, feelings, and assumptions that can provide a foundation for informed decision making.

Suggestion: If some participants grow impatient for action, it is useful to pause and for the group to ask itself whether more dialogue is needed or not. Sometimes a greater depth of mutual understanding is unnecessary for dealing with a practical problem, and under these conditions the dialogue *should* segue into a discussion of appropriate action. But sometimes the very nature of the problem is the lack of mutual understanding, and a premature rush to action can only worsen it. Inevitably, one or another participant will say, "What are we going to do about it?" If others then say something like "We are not quite ready for that yet. Let's hold it for just a bit," it usually helps to curb the group's impatience to move into action.

I was reminded of this reality in a series of dialogues in Canada. The participants, all Canadians except myself, expressed deep pessimism about ever reconciling the French- and English-speaking parts of Canada. Some were impatient for action now, of a separatist nature, and others were resigned fatalistically to an outcome in which the two cultures continued to drift apart in a climate of bitterness, resentment, and mutual recrimination.

All the participants were tired of the arguments and the debates that had raged unsuccessfully for almost a half century. But as they talked about the subject, it gradually dawned on them that despite all of the senseless political churning, the only people who had ever probed in depth the ways the two cultures can coexist had been a tiny handful of people at the highest levels of the Canadian government. The one strategy that had never been put to the test was genuine dialogue between average French- and English-speaking Canadians from all of the provinces. In the rush to action, the one indispensable step—achieving better mutual understanding—had been skipped.

In my experience, even hardheaded, practical-minded participants will curb their impatience for action if they themselves see that lack of mutual understanding is at the very heart of the problem that concerns them. Even though their temperament leads them away from talk toward activism, they begin to grasp the reality that sometimes dialogue *is* action.

4. *Listening Without Hearing*

One of the most common potholes is an unwillingness to make an extra effort to understand others when they are not wholly articulate. Most people, especially when conflict-ridden, are unaccustomed to finding the right words and phrases to express their feelings. Empathic listening requires patience and an ability to tune in to other people's feelings.

Actually hearing what other people are trying to say, as opposed to reacting to their literal words, is the exception rather than the rule. You would not be surprised, for example, if a woman friend said about her husband, "Well, he thinks he's listening to me, but he doesn't really hear what I'm trying to tell him. *He doesn't hear me.*" Intuitively, from your own experience, you know what your friend means. The picture your friend's lament conjures up is of two people engaged in intense conversation without understanding each other. Perhaps they are preoccupied with their own concerns or responding to the surface levels of meaning in the conversation. But neither is truly open to what the other is trying to convey. They are not really listening.

All of us have learned through personal experience that in talking about issues that affect our feelings and interests we must usually expect not to be heard. In our culture, not being heard is a conditioned response that is constantly reinforced. A typical first reaction to views that oppose your own is to assume that you are not being understood and therefore to restate your own position more insistently, in the hope that the force of your convictions will cause it to register. Since it rarely does, such conversations quickly reach an impasse: they get more intense, they wind down, or they move on to some other subject.

Suggestion: One useful technique for avoiding this pothole is for participants to paraphrase what they think they heard the other person say. Since people are used to being misunderstood, they respond in a highly positive fashion to evidence that they have been heard correctly and that their viewpoint is registering. Even if they have been misunderstood, the act of the other participants' playing back what they think they heard gives them the opportunity to correct or amplify their position. In good dialogue, a participant will often exclaim with appreciation, "Yes, that's just what I mean" or "That's one part of it, but I would like to add something." This process of ensuring that participants have heard one another correctly is one of the main sources of the warmth and good feeling that dialogues habitually generate. People appreciate being heard!

5. Starting at Different Points

Dialogue participants often find themselves at different stages in the judgment curve on an issue. This is one of the trickiest of all the potholes to deal with. In an earlier work I tracked seven stages in the process whereby people move from raw opinion to considered judgment on an issue.[1] In a typical dialogue, some participants are still in the earliest stages of working through their feelings, while others have resolved the issue for themselves. Value-laden issues take huge amounts of time to absorb, work through, and resolve thoughtfully.

Nothing expedites this laborious process better than good dialogue. But if participants find themselves at radically different stages of working through an issue, they will find it difficult to reach mutual understanding. I have encountered this obstacle on issues such as AIDS, drug abuse, health care reform, education reform, affirmative action, welfare, family stability, out-of-wedlock children, and many other emotion-laden issues.

Typically, participants enter with strong preexisting points of view. Also typically, their points of view are modified in the course of the dialogue. But if some participants have been thinking about the issue for years and others only for minutes, getting both categories of participants on the same wavelength is a tough problem.

Suggestion: In most dialogues, little effort is devoted to navigating this pothole for the simple reason that its depth and magnitude are rarely recognized. To the extent that the understanding gap is merely a matter of some participants being better informed than others, it is relatively easy to address. Some form of briefing can help immensely. For bringing participants up to speed, Public Agenda, for example, depends on special issue books. These present complex issues organized in the form of citizen choices for solution. Most people can find at least one choice that fits their values and preconceptions, freeing them to consider the pros and cons of other choices. An organization can utilize a wide range of briefing materials and presentations for this purpose or call upon the services of resource people who can fill in the information voids.

Often, however, the understanding gap cannot be bridged by information alone. The critical issue is whether or not participants have wrestled with the emotions that difficult issues raise, sometimes involving agonizing life-and-death choices. In the field of health care, for example, our society is currently struggling with the need to confront what is called "heroic medicine," strenuous efforts to prolong a dying person's life though technical means, at enormous financial and emotional cost. In dialogue on this subject, people invariably talk in terms of what they would do if their own loved ones were involved. Some people have courageously faced this issue and worked it through; most avoid thinking about it. Sustaining dialogue among people who would rather not confront an issue can be frustrating because there is so much denial to deal with. If people can avoid making painful decisions, they will. As the poet T. S. Eliot observed, people's capacity for reality is limited.

Addressing this kind of gap—between those who have worked through a painful issue and those who haven't—is always time-consuming. By sharing their feelings and experiences, those who have personally worked through the issue can help those who have not. The most practical way to deal with this obstacle is to allocate extra time for the dialogue and use it to invite those who are further along in the process of resolution to recount how and why their thoughts and feelings evolved, permitting those in earlier stages of resolution to ask them questions and compare experiences.

6. Showboating

We live in an era that places a high value on self-expression. Baby boomers, in particular, have grown up encouraged to express all facets of their personalities. Unhappily, doing dialogue can conflict with these urges: subordinating one's personality to a certain extent is needed to empathize fully with someone else's point of view. And this is not always easy to do.

Showboating is all too common even among the highest level of leaders. People, men in particular, can't resist the chance to show off how much they know, how smart they are, how tough-minded they can be, and how active they are as players in the game.

Academics are often the worst showboaters. One knows in advance that however thoroughly someone may have presented his or her point of view, some participants are going to start their comments with the words "You overlooked . . ." or "You failed to mention . . ."

Suggestion: If one knows in advance that certain participants have a tendency to showboat, it is advisable to add extra time for the dialogue. In most instances, the urge subsides once the showboaters have had a chance to express themselves. Having displayed their feathers in their full glory, they can then settle back and relax. There are, of course, some incorrigible showboaters who are so narcissistic that they must be "on" at all times. These types of people are not cut out for dialogue, and the only solution may be to wait patiently until they play themselves out.

7. Scoring Debating Points

Many participants in dialogue are trained as adversaries and find it difficult to park their old habits at the door. They listen attentively, but not for the purpose of understanding; their impulse is to rebut. If another participant has stated a point poorly or overstated it, their response is not to make the extra effort to learn what the speaker really means; it is to pounce on the ill-chosen words and tear holes in the argument.

This style is not confined to lawyers. It also characterizes advocacy groups, political activists, diplomats, labor and management representatives, and other professionals. It mirrors the lopsidedness of our culture, with its stress on competition rather than cooperation.

Suggestion: Here, too, it is advisable to add extra time to dialogue sessions. People who habitually adopt the adversarial mode do so out of temperament, training, and habit. They know the rules of that game and play it well. Often, however, they are responsive to the suggestion that dialogue is a different kind of game, one that requires setting aside one's adversarial weaponry (a suggestion best made before the dialogue begins so that it does not imply criticism). But ingrained habits are not easily suspended. So time must be allotted to permit outbursts of debate that less adversarial participants can gradually guide back into the dialogic mode of discourse.

8. Contrarianism

Contrarianism is a similar kind of pothole. There are some people who can't help adopting a contrary point of view. They automatically advance an argument—often a compelling one—that takes the opposite stance from one that has just been taken. For them, dialogue is a game of wits. They enjoy the sport of it and are often superb in its performance. Certainly, fireworks and controversy make for a livelier game than the quiet and probably more boring (from a sporting point of view) pursuit of mutual understanding.

Suggestion: If there is ample time, contrarianism can add value to a dialogue. It does so by expanding the range of possible explanations, ideas, and choices. Of course, it demands of participants an extra measure of patience, especially if the contrarianism is a form of sport or self-indulgence. But if participants are hanging tough on their fixed positions, new contrarian perspectives may help to break up old patterns of thought. And if contrarian participants become obstructive, other participants (or a facilitator) can guide them back to dialogue.

9. Having a Pet Preoccupation

Many people are obsessed with some single idea or interest, so much so that they cannot get it out of their minds long enough to entertain ideas that do not take their preoccupation into account. Such *idées fixes* prevent people from hearing what others have to say.

When I was growing up in a Jewish neighborhood in Boston, residents were obsessed with the question "Is it good for the Jews?" At school, we used to play a game parodying this tendency by composing fictitious titles for newspaper or magazine articles such as "South Africa's Dwindling Elephant Population and the Jewish Question" or "Vast Oil Reserves Discovered in Latin America and How This Affects the Jews." I confess that I am often reminded of this game at meetings when participants get hung up on comparable preoccupations. The popular ones these days revolve around gender, race, political correctness, the oppressiveness of government regulations, the corruptness of campaign financing, and the varied sins of the media. (It is a rare dialogue in which someone does not blame the media for every conceivable defect in our society.)

The issue here is not whether these preoccupations are justified; many of them are. I am simply making the point that they form a huge pothole that blocks the way to open oneself up to the concerns, ideas, and values of others.

Suggestion: This is a relatively easy pothole to navigate. Participants with a pet preoccupation are usually convinced that others are unaware of the importance of the point they wish to make. Therefore, it is important that they be given the chance to articulate, even repeat, their concern. But often this will not be enough. Other participants must repeatedly show that they truly understand the point and take it seriously, even if they don't agree with it.

Realistically, the process may require several iterations before the person with the pet preoccupation takes in the fact that he or she has in fact been heard and understood.

10. Aria Singing

A related obstacle is the compulsion some leaders feel to push their constituents' interests rather than to heed the concerns of the other dialogue participants. By definition, a leader comes with followers. For a leader, it is not easy to resist the temptation to advance the special interests of those he or she represents, however ill-timed or disruptive to the dialogue they may be.

Many a dialogue has been sidetracked by the special pleading of a well-meaning leader. We live in an era of identity politics; group consciousness is not easily set aside. The leaders of minorities, the women's movement, environmentalists, religious groups, and those at the extremes of the political spectrum are prone to singing their arias at the slightest provocation—or even without any provocation.

Suggestion: The same considerations that apply to Showboating (No. 6) and Pet Preoccupations (No. 9) apply here as well.

LEARNING TO AVOID THE POTHOLES

The chances are that people who habitually find themselves stumbling into these kinds of potholes will not learn to avoid them merely by having them identified in a book. A number of the potholes are created by personality characteristics that are not readily changed. Some people have imperative ego needs over which they have imperfect control, even when they are aware of the negative way others react to them. Those who do not have personality hang-ups may have a tin ear from inexperience or inattention. Those with a technical orientation may not have focused on strengthening other capabilities in their lives, so that when they are thrust into situations that call for sensitive interpersonal skills, they may falter badly.

There are two strategies that dialogue groups can pursue to minimize the effects of these kinds of potholes, and happily, they are complementary. Either one, or a combination of the two, can greatly improve both individuals' dialogic skills and the abilities of the dialogue group to skirt the potholes.

One strategy is to seek individual training. There exist a number of organizations designed precisely to assist individuals to become more effective in their people-to-people relationships. In the US, these include the Delta Consulting Group (New York), Blessing White (Princeton), Landmark

Education Inc. (San Francisco), and JMW (Stamford, Connecticut). These and other consultants across the world have developed programs that fill a huge gap in education/training systems. Typically, we receive our professional training in substantive areas such as engineering, journalism, or medicine. But immersion in a professional discipline prepares one poorly in the skills required to work effectively with others.

Typically, a first-rate bench chemist in a company, a high-performance salesperson, or an exceptionally capable financial analyst will learn that he or she has been promoted to a managerial position that starts immediately. Such people's first reaction is delight with their new status, but the delight quickly turns to anxiety when they discover that while their technical skills are excellent, their people-managing skills are deficient. Consulting organizations that specialize in training are highly effective in helping people compensate for this lopsidedness in their backgrounds. The consultants' success rate is remarkably high because they are usually working with capable, well-motivated people who happen to lack specific people skills, often due to inattention or neglect. Though not many currently offer programs focused specifically on dialogic skills, they are likely to do so in the future.

A complementary strategy is aimed not at the individual but at the dialogic group itself. It is, in effect, a form of on-the-job learning for the group. Groups can learn about both strategies and potholes in the context of ongoing dialogues. Some groups can do this on their own. Others will benefit from using a skilled facilitator to help them learn how to apply dialogue strategies and avoid potholes.

For potholes related to participants' ego needs, on-the-job group learning is particularly effective. If someone needs to show how smart he is, he may settle down after he has had a few chances to show off to the rest of the group. If he has a pet preoccupation, it will recede into the background if he has a chance to ventilate it and the group shows itself responsive to his concerns. In either case, if the disruptive behavior does not diminish, the group or its facilitator can call attention to it constructively and then guide the group back to the path of dialogue.

Other potholes also lend themselves to repair within the dialogue group. Participants who tend to hold back can be encouraged to give of themselves if others turn to them and elicit their views. Members of the group can learn to impose a certain discipline by reminding those who insist upon making debating points or who leap prematurely into action about the strategies appropriate to dialogue. In fact, the people who habitually stumble into these potholes sometimes turn out to be among the best dialogue participants once they learn of the inappropriateness (for dialogue) of their response patterns.

The dialogue process itself may be the best training ground for those who appear to listen without really hearing and for those whose thinking remains constricted ("thinking within a box"). The exercise of hearing yourself speak your own assumptions out loud and listening to others respond to them is, for most participants, an immensely broadening experience. If someone isn't truly listening, it becomes obvious to the rest of the group, some of whom will, more or less tactfully, point this out. People do not like being shamed in the presence of their peers; after a few times they begin to listen more attentively. For the most narrow thinkers within the group, the experience of hearing others who bring broader points of view to bear is often an eye-opening experience: there is probably no better way to broaden one's horizons.

The major drawback to these forms of on-the-job training

is that they take time and commitment. They are, therefore, inappropriate for casual groups that do dialogue only once on an ad hoc basis. But they work well within institutions and organizations comprising people who work together over extended periods of time.

PART III

THE BROADER USES OF DIALOGUE

Chapter 9

Cultural Fault Lines

To see the magic of dialogue at its fullest and most powerful, we now shift our gaze from individuals and organizations to the larger society. We are living through a moment in history when dialogue offers us a unique opportunity to address a series of problems that are jeopardizing the quality of American civilization.

There is a web of fault lines in our culture, stresses that lie deep beneath the surface of daily life. There are three major fault lines, all interconnected, and dialogue is useful in compensating for all of them.

"I-It" Is Growing

Martin Buber has found a succinct way to distinguish between two modes of relating to others: I-It and I-Thou. The I-Thou relationship is a direct, highly personal form of reaching out to others and opening oneself to them. The I-It relationship distances people; it is more impersonal, more remote, more objectifying. In our culture, we tend to depersonalize people, to distance ourselves from one another, to fall all too easily into the I-It mode.

In the I-Thou relationship the distance between I and Thou

vanishes. We are no longer separated by status, social propriety, self-consciousness, one-upmanship, indifference, aloofness, self-protectiveness, or well-meaning good manners. We encounter one another as persons; we speak to one another directly, without distance.

Buber's I-It/I-Thou language will strike some readers as old-fashioned, even archaic. For a long time, that was my own reaction. But personal experience caused me to change my mind and the evocative power of Buber's categories has grown on me. After Mary, my young wife, was killed in an automobile accident, I soon became inured to the many expressions of condolence I received from people whom I knew only casually. All offered their sympathies with sincerity, but I was conscious of the discomfort and distance most felt in bringing up such a painful and awkward subject. I squirmed at the self-conscious remoteness between us, responding politely but keeping my own distance.

I remember, however, a handful of occasions when someone's sympathy moved me deeply. One occurred several months after Mary's death. I was eating lunch at an Aspen Institute picnic in Aspen, Colorado. A new official of the institute, to whom I had just been introduced, came up to me, sat on the rock beside me, and shortly after we began to speak asked me what it was like living alone without Mary. There was nothing eloquent or special about the words themselves, but everything in his tone, his body language, his physical closeness, his entire being expressed an unself-conscious reaching out. There are many forms of I-Thou relationship. For me, this was one.

The I-It relationship, by contrast, removes people from one another in countless ways. It is in play whenever people are seen as objects, as, for example, when a surgeon refers to a patient as the "infarction in Room 379," when an executive thinks of employees as "my people" or "labor," when scientists describe a group of subjects as "the control group."

Anthropologist Clifford Geertz notes that his own field has traditionally been dominated by a "me-anthropologist-you-native" mind-set. In this type of communication, anthropologists interpose a vast social distance between themselves and those they study.[1]

Depersonalizing people is not new to our culture. But the spread of expertise, professionalism, commercialism, and technology has greatly expanded its scope. The press of daily transactions, most of them impersonal, causes us to deal with each other at arm's length. Increasingly, the transactions take on an edge of rudeness, a lack of civility. We all complain about the explosion of bad manners. (For example, three out of five Americans [61%][2] think of their fellow Americans as rude, and four out of five [77%][3] see the lack of courtesy and manners in everyday American life as a serious problem.) In our public lives and, to some extent, even our private lives, the I-It mode has swollen, while the I-Thou mode has shrunk.

The undesirable side effects of this trend have their greatest impact on public rather than private life: in our families and friendships, we still manage to treat each other as persons rather than objects. But in our encounters with institutions, professionals, and public policy, its effects convey the loss of respect that so troubles us.

My firm's research shows that most of us harbor an unsatisfied hunger for community: a place where people know about you, care about you, where you belong. In the conditions of the twenty-first century, we cannot reproduce the communities of the nineteenth-century small town. But through dialogue we can penetrate the veneer that has been created by too many impersonal transactions. There is a middle ground between the intimacy of deeply personal relationships and the impersonality (and increasing rudeness) of day-to-day transactions.

Imagine, for example, Professor Geertz modifying his style of doing anthropology to reflect his conviction that the very language of anthropology (and the other social sciences) approaches subjects as if they were objects and his recognition that this kind of I-It relationship is demeaning to the people being studied. Sensitized by this realization, Geertz and other anthropologists learn to speak even to the most exotic tribespeople on an equal footing, as one human being to another. They thus shift from the scientific observer (I-It) mode into the human dialogue (I-Thou) mode.

THE SILO EFFECT IS SPREADING

A second fault line might be called "the silo effect"—the tendency of our culture to fragment itself into subcultures so removed from one another as to isolate us into an aggregation of silos.

People are locked into frameworks peculiar to their own subcultures and are unable—or unwilling—to break out of them. Journalists develop interests that increasingly distance them from the public. Educators dismiss appeals to teach work-related skills as mere "vocationalism" that cheapens their mission. Physicians committed to preserving life at all costs are herded into the hostile subculture of managed care, which undermines a professional ethic carefully nurtured over decades. Not only are colleges and universities cut off from the larger society, but the silos within the academic specialties are also isolated from one another. I have listened for hours to economists and psychologists, historians and sociologists, biologists and scholars in the humanities argue with each other without either penetrating the subculture of the other. It is almost as if these subcultures were gated communities of the mind, now spreading as rapidly as the literal kind of gated community.

A number of years ago, Britain's C. P. Snow deplored the magnitude of the gap separating the sciences from the humanities. Not only has the divide between the two cultures grown wider since Snow's time, but within the humanities a chaos of subcultures flourishes. Even within science, physicists often have difficulty communicating with mathematicians, and within mathematics, with its eighty-four or so subspecialties, few individual mathematicians pay heed to more than two or three.

Fragmentation is so prevalent that to make connections between subcultures we must resort to what anthropologists call "cross-cultural communication"—the kind of semantic bridge building needed when people literally come from different cultures. The Japanese psychiatrist Takeo Doi recounts a personal example of the misunderstandings that arise under these conditions. He writes that in his first visit to America, he arrived for an overnight stay at the home of an American colleague. He was greeted by his colleague's wife, who told him he was welcome and then urged him to feel free "to help himself" during his stay. On hearing these words, Doi says, he was overcome by a wave of loneliness and isolation; in Japan, under no circumstances would honored guests be asked to help themselves; every courtesy and form of help are extended to them.[4] Thus, a warm, familiar gesture of welcome and generosity in a Western context is translated in a Japanese context into a gesture of rejection. Dr. Doi and his hostess were carrying on a conversation but not a dialogue; they were not understanding each other.

You don't have to come from another culture to misunderstand each other, as psycholinguist Deborah Tannen makes clear in *You Just Don't Understand,* her best-selling book about how men and women in our own culture chronically fail to communicate with each other. Dr. Tannen observes that males and females, even in the same household, are raised in worlds so distinct from each other that talk between the sexes falls into the technical category of cross-cultural communication.[5]

As a consequence of social change, relationships between men and women in our society are undergoing revolutionary changes. Our research shows that many women feel they have achieved many of the goals they set for themselves in the 1960s, such as greater independence and fairer treatment in the workplace. But independence has come at a cost. Two thirds of women living alone (66%) say they are beset by loneliness.[6] Personal relations between men and women have been thrown into disarray. Men, in particular, feel confused and uncertain. Deborah Tannen's title, *You Just Don't Understand,* is poignantly apt. In today's culture, ordinary conversation between men and women isn't enough to ensure mutual understanding or the ability to relate to each other in an I-Thou mode.

Dialogue is a simple, straightforward way to bridge these cultural fault lines. Imagine a conversation, for example, that might take place a few days after Dr. Doi is disconcerted by the suggestion that he ought to help himself. He confesses his discomfort to his hostess. He tells her that a friend has explained to him that the real meaning of the phrase "Just help yourself" is a desire for the guest to feel as if he were in his own home and that it does not have the meaning he attributed to it of "You're on your own, buddy. Don't expect any help from us." The hostess is momentarily flustered by the mis-

understanding but soon finds herself laughing over the incident. In a tiny way, sharing and then clarifying the misunderstanding brings hostess and guest closer together. Their
conversation has evolved into dialogue.

THERE IS TOO MUCH TOP-DOWN TALK

The third fault line in our culture is the chasm of misunderstanding and miscommunication that separates the nation's
elites from the general public. It is the most serious of the
three and the most difficult to contain. It doesn't affect dialogue among the leaders themselves, but it plays havoc with
relationships between leaders and their constituencies, making it difficult for our society to adopt dialogue as an easy,
comfortable, and effective way for elites and the public to
carry out the public's business.

This is a fault line of long standing. At the end of political
scientist V. O. Key's book *Public Opinion and American
Democracy,* Key expresses his concern that the divide between
elites and the general public is the most vulnerable aspect of
our nation's democracy. (By "elites," Key means not only government officials but also "influentials" such as media pundits, well-placed lawyers and judges, leading intellectuals and
scientists, the top military brass, the medical establishment,
community leaders, and experts of various kinds.) If our
democracy ever falls apart, he believes that it is most likely to
do so along this divide.[7]

Widening and deepening the divide is our culture's overreliance on a one-way, top-down model of communication
("top-down talk"). The antithesis of dialogue, top-down talk
is largely responsible for the effects that the average person

experiences as lack of respect. Today's world of predominantly top-down talk converts the public into passive targets of messages that cause them to feel they are not being treated as thinking, independent individuals.

Overreliance on top-down talk takes a number of subtly different forms. One is that of the expert professional: "I, the professional, know things you don't know. As a doctor, I know medicine. As a journalist, I know what is and isn't newsworthy. As an investment adviser, I know the world of stocks and bonds. As an educator, I know how to teach students what they need to know. I am willing to impart a tiny fraction of my knowledge to you, the public. And I want to do everything possible to make my position clear and understandable. But since you are not trained to be a doctor (or journalist, investor, or educator), there isn't anything you can contribute back to me."

Another form is that of the policy maker: "We have gone to a great deal of trouble to shape a policy that meets your needs, is practical and affordable, and also meets the requirements of various special interests. Since this is a democracy and we are ultimately accountable to the will of the people, we want to make sure that you are well informed about the policy so that you can support it."

Yet another form is that of the employer: "You are our loyal and dedicated employees—our company's most valuable asset. We are willing to go to great lengths to inform you of the company's policies and to answer any questions you may have, but we don't expect you to contribute to our thinking."

There are countless variants, but all share the assumption that it is the task of the leader or expert to convey the message and the task of recipients of the message to understand and absorb it, *not* to contribute to its content. Top-down talk dominates our communications and is driving a dangerous wedge between leaders and the public.

Minimizing the Damage

The three fault lines are symptoms of the same underlying malady, a deeply disturbing tendency I have described in other works as a "culture of technical control."[8] This a mind-set, all-pervasive in our culture (especially in managerial and professional circles), that treats people as objects to be manipulated. It seeks to control people, circumstances, and life itself. In our daily lives, we are most exposed to this practice through political spin doctoring, social engineering, bureaucratic organization, government regulation, and the kind of corporate downsizing we associate with professional managers such as "Chainsaw Al" Dunlop. Whole libraries of books of philosophy, politics, sociology, and postmodern literary criticism are devoted to identifying and critiquing this deep-rooted distortion in our culture.

Significantly, dialogue has an important role to play in countering the negative effects of this destructive tendency. Dialogue can serve as a powerful corrective for all three fault lines. It can move us away from I-It toward I-Thou. It can build connections among the silos of our subculture isolation. And it can narrow the elite–public gap.

But it can't have these positive effects unless we develop a deliberate strategy to make it happen. Fortunately, the task is simplified to some degree because we do not need three separate strategies, one for each fault line. The three are so closely intertwined that a strategy for curbing the damage caused by any one of them will be effective (with minor variations) with the other two as well.

In the next few chapters, I focus on a strategy to reverse the damage caused by the third fault line: the elite–public gap. It is the most concrete of the three and therefore the easiest to keep in focus. And it is the most threatening to the practice of democracy because it alienates the public and leads to apathy, low voter turnout, and growing mistrust of government and other institutions.

Devising an effective strategy will not be easy. Powerful resistances and blind spots prevent elites from engaging the public in dialogue. They don't see any good reason to do so, and even if they did, there are no well-established methods for conducting dialogue between leaders and the general public. This combination of lack of will and lack of know-how poses a formidable obstacle.

Our society's discomfort with carrying out leader–public dialogues falls into the category of intractable problems I have come to think of as "will/skill dilemmas." Some problems resist solution because the will to solve them is lacking. Others resist solution because the know-how to solve them is lacking. The worst kinds of problems are those cursed with both lack of will *and* lack of skill, creating a vicious cycle: skills remain undeveloped because of low motivation, and motivation doesn't kick in because of lack of skills. This double bind is a classic formula for inaction, and it blocks the use of dialogue to narrow or eliminate the expert–public gap in Western culture.

Fortunately, our chances of devising a strategy for overcoming this particular will/skill dilemma are much better now than in the recent past. A decade ago they were bleak, but now they are more promising for reasons we will discuss in the next few chapters.

Chapter 10

Proxy Dialogue

To clear the path for dialogue to play a more important role in our public life, two strategies are required: one for the will side of the will/skill dilemma, another for the skill side. The strategies for each are very different: a strategy for the skill side involves developing new models of communication, while a strategy for the will side involves overcoming massive leadership resistance.

It is best to start with a strategy for the skill side. There is little point in asking leaders to engage the public in dialogue if they draw a blank on how to do so. The missing skill is a matter not of leadership ignorance but of inappropriate models of communication. Except for the Internet, most existing models are best suited to one-way communication. Under present circumstances, even with the best will in the world leaders would be hard put to engage the general public in serious and effective dialogue.

Public Dialogue on Social Security

The skill problem is largely a practical one. Dialogue is easiest to pull off with small groups of, say, twelve to thirty people. How, then, can hundreds, thousands, even millions of people participate in meaningful dialogue? How much loss is there when the scale of dialogue is vastly increased to include such large numbers of people? If the scale is increased, can the essential benefits of dialogue still be retained? What techniques work best, and what techniques merely give the appearance of dialogue without its substance? These are difficult questions. But there are surprisingly positive answers to all of them, even though some do not conform to the conventional wisdom.

The single biggest obstacle is the sheer size of the groups that should participate in dialogue. The larger the group, the harder it is to visualize methods for permitting its leaders and members to enter into genuine dialogue with one another. Nor will this problem disappear or lessen in the future. On the contrary; the issue of size and scale is likely to grow ever more serious as the population grows larger and more diverse.

To confront the issue head-on, let us consider the most difficult challenge of all: the need for dialogue on issues that concern the entire population. There are a number of such issues, for example, managing the costs, quality and availability of health care in an aging population; reforming schools so they can provide the skills young people need in a global economy; dealing constructively with the race issue, especially in the inner cities; and protecting Social Security so that it remains viable for the twenty-first century.

The future of Social Security is an excellent test of the feasibility of large-scale public dialogue. Social Security affects everyone, and the issues it raises cry out for the kind of public discourse that only dialogue can deliver. Indeed, without the "working through" that dialogue can uniquely achieve, the conflicts associated with protecting Social Security in an aging population may be left unresolved.

On issues such as Social Security, we need a new communication model for public dialogue, and in what follows I outline a bare-bones sketch of one. It will require extensive experimentation, but our culture is so well endowed with gifted communications professionals that once a direction is indicated, they will know how to implement it skillfully and creatively.

An important first step is to gain a sound research-based understanding of the issue from the public's perspective. My research, and that of others, shows unmistakably that the public has grown increasingly anxious about the future of Social Security. This anxiety affects young and old alike. Pensioners feel they have earned their benefits by paying their taxes and are fearful that these benefits may be cut, leaving them bereft. They therefore see any reduction in benefits as a form of theft. Younger people are cynical and fearful at the same time: they are convinced that when their turn comes, the system will be bankrupt and all the money they are now paying in Social Security taxes will have disappeared.

Our political leaders therefore assume that the public is sharply divided along generational lines. If the huge baby-boom generation is ever to enjoy the benefits of Social Security, today's pensioners must make some concessions, and our elected officials fear that they are not willing to do so. Our political leaders visualize hordes of vengeful senior citizens with time on their hands lying in wait to destroy any politician who proposes even modest sacrifices for the sake of future generations.

But the assumption that an irreconcilable conflict of interest divides the young and the old is not, in fact, valid. Our research reveals that the conflict of economic interests between the generations is far weaker than the mutuality of concern that each generation feels toward the other. Younger people worry about their parents and other older people, and older people worry that the younger generation may not get its due. The fierce glare of politics blinds us to the strength of the civility that still underlies mainstream life, even though it is now being frayed.

Of course, economic self-interest influences people's actions, but self-interest is not the only motivation that counts. It only seems that way because of the mistrust that pervades the issue. The Social Security problem looks insoluble only if approached from a traditional top-down leadership posture: finesse the problem, hammer out a technical fix among interest groups and leaders, and sell it to a public preoccupied solely with its own economic self-interest.

The same problem that threatens an impasse from a top-down talk point of view looks resolvable when examined from a dialogic point of view. A solution based on mutuality of sacrifice and benefit can be hammered out that will be acceptable to both the younger and older generations.

In this situation dialogue is absolutely necessary to increase mutual understanding, reduce mistrust, dispel stereotypes, bring assumptions into the open where they can be examined and corrected, find the common ground that unites people's concerns rather than focus on the differences that divide them, and above all give the public the time it needs to digest and work through the various proposals for resolving the conflicts associated with Social Security reform.

A National Dialogue

We come now to the all-important second step: how to conduct such a dialogue. There are a bewildering number of options:

- Should we, for example, organize vast numbers of dialogues among mini–citizen groups throughout the country, coordinated with the editorial support of local newspapers and TV stations?
- Should we respond to the promise of the new communication technology and try to conduct the dialogue on the Internet?
- Should we mobilize the nation's experts as television's talking heads to explain the issues to the public?
- Should we conduct a series of televised "town hall" meetings between leaders and representatives of the public?

Unfortunately, none of these options is equal to the task. Each has crippling drawbacks. Consider the option involving thousands of dialogues among minigroups of citizens and leaders in communities all over the nation. The magnitude and scale of such an effort make it awesome to contemplate but not impossible to implement. The killer drawback, I fear, is not the huge scale of the effort but the likelihood that genuine dialogue would not take place in such meetings. There are not enough knowledgeable and open-minded leaders to go around to participate in all of the meetings. Also, multiple meetings of the same groups would be required; a single meeting would simply compound the confusion about Social Security that now exists. Most importantly, if the central thesis of this book—namely, that dialogue requires training in special skills—is correct, those skills will be absent from most of the meetings and the media involvement with them. This approach can be made to work on a small scale, but not on a large one. It works only if special attention can be lavished on each meeting. Special attention can be lavished on a handful of such meetings, not on tens of thousands of them.

With regard to using the Internet for dialogue, the Internet *does* open new possibilities for citizen–leader interaction. But today it is available mainly to the college-educated minority It is not yet a universal medium like television or the telephone. Also, the impersonal nature of interaction on the Net raises serious questions that will need to be addressed and explored further. There may be satisfactory answers to them, but at the moment they remain unknown.

The third option—mobilizing the nation's experts as talking heads on television—would, if my thesis in this book is sound, set us back rather than move us forward. Whatever benefits top-down talk from experts may produce, the advancement of dialogue between public and leaders is not one of them.

The fourth option—extensive use of televised "town hall" meetings—seems plausible but in practice has shown itself to be deeply flawed as a vehicle for dialogue. Our political leaders have tried this approach on a number of occasions, with mediocre results at best. The disappointing failure of so-called town hall meetings to advance genuine dialogue has many causes. One is that they violate a core principle of dialogue: the need to ensure equality of standing among all participants. In the televised town hall meetings I have observed between the president of the United States and average citizens, true dialogue has been strikingly absent. These town hall meetings contain elements of showmanship, debate, Q and A, special pleading, showboating, didactic instruction, and pyrotechnics; everything but the quiet seriousness of give-and-take that is characteristic of dialogue among equals.

Proxy Dialogue

If these and similar approaches won't work, what will? I am convinced that television is the only practical medium for conducting mass public dialogue and that a certain kind of televised dialogue can reproduce many of the benefits of small-group dialogue. TV is the source of most people's daily intake of information and entertainment, and it exercises a vast influence on the public.

At first glance, television appears to have a decisive drawback for dialogue because, with the questionable exception of call-in talk shows, it is not interactive. But if one analyzes TV's influence on the public, it becomes clear that television can achieve the effects of interactivity without literally requiring viewers and TV performers to interact with one another.

There are a number of instructive examples. One is Bill Moyers's US television series on the Book of Genesis. Moyers invited a small group of theologians to discuss the meaning of the Genesis story. The televised discussion unfolded in a relaxed and informal fashion, with flashes of tension at moments of disagreement. The Moyers inquiry sought neither consensus nor conflict; the conversation flowed naturally as each of the participants explored his or her own feelings about the biblical story.

One of the most striking aspects of the series—striking because it is so rare on TV—was the responsiveness of the participants to one another. The conversation was not the usual series of solo performances interspersed with the host's witty jibes or challenges. It was a real conversation in the sense that the participants listened to one another and responded appropriately.

At frequent intervals the conversation evolved into genuine dialogue, with the participants listening empathically to one another, treating one another as equals, and raising assumptions in a nonjudgmental fashion. Judith Moyers (the coproducer) told me that the audience response to the series had been phenomenal, with many thousands of viewers writing cards and letters. Viewers were riveted to the programs because they found themselves able to identify with one or more of the participants on a subject that profoundly engaged them. Each viewer discovered a dialogue participant who articulated the responses, questions, convictions, and reactions that they themselves were experiencing.

Or consider a very different kind of example: the televised debates in Congress on the eve of the Persian Gulf War in 1991. President George Bush had decided to send American troops into Kuwait to repel Saddam Hussein's invasion and to force the Iraqis back to their own borders. I recall Congress's reaction vividly because it was so unusual. As members of Congress spoke, instead of making the usual lawyerlike arguments for their point of view, they eloquently expressed their own torn feelings: anxiety about putting American soldiers in harm's way conflicting with the need to counter the Iraqi threat to vital American interests and world peace.

If the congressional response had been the usual partisan debate, it would not have made a dent on the public's sensibilities. But when our political leaders put aside their trained adversarial tendencies and instead responded like ordinary humans, openly expressing their concerns, the impact on the public was extraordinary. Average US citizens saw and heard their leaders struggling with the same mixed feelings that they themselves were experiencing. Because members of Congress articulated these feelings with clarity and eloquence—and because they also expressed their conclusions after working through their conflicting emotions—they helped the public to resolve its own ambivalence. The result was massive public support for the kind of military action the public would ordinarily reject because of its Vietnam-like character: open-ended American military engagement in a Third World hot spot.

In both instances, the extraordinary impact on the public

came from the power of identification. The ability of viewers to form a bond of identification with TV performers is the source of television's great influence. Walter Cronkite, the former anchorman on *The CBS Evening News,* was often said to be the most trusted man in America because average viewers were able to identify with him. Oprah Winfrey and Larry King derive their enormous influence from their ability to create strong personal identification between viewers and themselves. Indeed, moments of genuine dialogue occur on both of their shows.

It is identification that makes mass televised dialogue possible. We can, therefore, harness the power of identification through a form of televised dialogue we might call "proxy dialogue." This is dialogue that takes place among groups of people on television with whom viewers identify so closely that they are able to serve as proxies. What now happens on television sporadically and occasionally can be made to happen almost routinely—if certain principles are observed.

The first principle is that dialogue participants must faithfully express the concerns and values of most of the population. We have seen that viewers can identify with almost anyone who expresses values and feelings comparable to their own. These proxies might be professional TV personalities or leaders who are able to speak in a nontechnical manner, or they might be members of the general public. (One might think that call-in shows would yield good public representation, but ironically, call-in shows offer the least promising potential for creating dialogue. This is because the people who call in almost never represent the views of the majority. Most people are very reluctant to pick up the telephone and call in to a radio or TV talk show. Those who do usually speak for the most opinionated fringes of the political spectrum.)

The second principle is that it is essential to meet the three core requirements of dialogue: empathic listening, equality of standing, and nonjudgmental surfacing of assumptions. At this stage of our inquiry, no further elaboration of this point is needed.

The third principle, also discussed earlier, is that program planners will have to conduct sufficient viewer research before using televised dialogue to present issues such as Social Security from the public's perspective rather than from the perspective of a technical expert, a partisan political leader, a self-seeking interest group, or the current crop of television producers, who insist on staging conflict and confrontation because of their supposedly superior entertainment value.

An important fourth principle is that television dialogues should not seek to reproduce the sprawling, disorganized, and repetitive character of real-life dialogue. The medium of television imposes a rigorous discipline. Experienced documentary producers, for example, observe this discipline by shooting ten to twenty hours of film for every one they use. The editing process is the most arduous aspect of television. The same principle applies to proxy dialogue: it may well take twenty hours of filmed dialogue to edit down into a single hour or even half hour of televised dialogue.

A moment's reflection on these four principles will show that proxy dialogue is no more demanding or difficult than many current forms of TV production. It is not a radical departure from present practice but merely a new application of a familiar technique.

Chapter 11

The Blind Spot and Other Resistances

When we turn now to a strategy for strengthening the political will of leaders to conduct dialogue with the public, we encounter a different kind of challenge. Our skill-side strategy proposed transferring the process of dialogue to television. In this shifting from interpersonal to proxy dialogue, there are, of course, inevitable trade-offs: for example, in the new format immediacy is lost but breadth is gained. In proxy dialogue, people are exposed to perspectives and points of view they ordinarily would not find in their limited circle of family, friends, and associates. On balance, proxy dialogue holds the promise of becoming a highly successful format for conducting public dialogue between leaders and large groups of people.

What about the will side? What is the objective we want to mobilize the political will to achieve? It is to find a way to give the public a greater say in shaping policies that affect their lives. The goal is to use dialogue as a lever for moving our society toward new forms of public engagement.

Unfortunately, success in achieving this goal depends on our ability to find ways around a huge obstacle, namely, the resistance of elites to doing dialogue with the public. Their resistance is unmistakable: they don't want to do it, and they see no logically compelling reasons why they should. Of course, leaders give lip service to the desirability of dialogue with the public. But the reality is that it imposes on them an onerous burden of time and effort and, from their perspective, has no obvious payoff. In short, the political will is just about nil.

Nonetheless, the picture is not as discouraging as these attitudes might suggest. Powerful forces at work in the society are pressuring elites to develop a more dialogic relationship with the public. Also, when we dig beneath the surface attitudes of elites' resistance, we find grounds for hope.

Elites' resistance has two sources. One is a fear of losing status through sharing the power of policy making with the mass public. The other is a blind spot—an unthinking assumption that the public's views are so ill informed, narrowly self-interested, unrealistic, and moralistic that they cannot add anything of value to the decision-making process.

Any hope for mobilizing the political will to engage the public directly in policy-shaping dialogue depends on a strategy that will address this formidable resistance head-on.

THE FEAR OF LOSS OF STATUS AND POWER

Elites are reluctant to enter into any transaction with the public that gives the public equal standing with them. They fear they will lose status and power by doing so. By definition, elites don't feel that the mass public is equal to them. They are willing to impart knowledge to the public because in doing so they retain—and reinforce—their status. But entering into dialogue with the public where all participants are equal is a way of saying to people, "Your views are as good as mine."

And elites do not feel that the public's views *are* as good as theirs.

Shaping policy is an important prerogative of status and power. Suppose, for example, you are an employer who decides to reduce expenses by replacing full-time, full-benefit workers with part-timers. You may be obliged to confront the union if the plant is unionized, and you will want to explain to core workers whom you retain on the full-time payroll the reasons for the policy shift and what it means to them. But if you are a typical employer you will see little point in entering into extensive dialogue with them. Doing so would diminish your own prerogatives as a manager by seeming to share decision making with workers.

In the past, leaders felt little need for dialogue with their constituents, employees, or customers. Whether they were autocratic, paternalistic, or simply accustomed to making decisions on their own, they could take for granted a respect for authority that led people to accept their decisions without insisting on being consulted.

In today's society, however, automatic respect for authority can no longer be taken for granted. Whether they be voters or employees or consumers, the average person is less willing than in earlier generations to respond to authority passively. People today are more insistent on their right to be heard.

In recent years, managers and officials have adapted to these trends and have evolved new models of leadership, especially in large business corporations where authoritarian models of leadership were once the norm. Experts in this field refer to the traditional model as command-and-control leadership (in analogy with the military model). In the command-and-control format, top-level executives set objectives and strategies and rely on the familiar carrot-and-stick approach for implementing them. The carrot is a blend of money, career advancement, and security. The stick is fear. These patterns of incentives and disincentives are familiar and deeply entrenched.

But experience has shown that they do not work well for certain types of institutions—those whose success depends on innovation, swift response to change, and highly motivated people who share the same vision and values. These institutions have found that money and fear can motivate people to do many things (e.g., follow orders) but they are not the best ways to stimulate creativity, innovation, commitment, and putting customers first (whether the customers are consumers, voters, workers, constituents, medical patients, or students).

In recent years a whole library of books and articles have devoted themselves to articulating new conceptions of leadership. The main difference between the older command-and-control and the newer leadership models lies in the assumptions each makes about the best way to mobilize people to achieve an institution's objectives.

Emerging models of leadership place their emphasis on cooperating, conducting dialogue, crossing boundaries, seeking alignment on a shared vision, tolerating complexity, and developing networks of relationships. I refer to this new conception as "relational leadership" because building relationships is so central to its success. The concept of relational leadership is still in its infancy, but it is rapidly evolving. Relational leadership is concerned primarily with change: establishing a direction for the organization (based on a vision of the future) and mobilizing the people, ideas, and resources needed to move in the desired direction.

Until recently, the trend toward more cooperative, relationship-building, dialogic models of leadership has had a fringe-like, New Age character. But mainstream companies and other institutions are now moving tentatively in this direction. As they do so, the search for new models of leadership that emphasize dialogue as a way of building relationships (as distinct from impersonal transactions) is shifting from the margins of life to its center.

In the command-and-control model, power is a zero-sum game: when you give power to others, you diminish your own power. In the relational leadership model, you do not diminish your power by sharing it. Indeed, power is not at issue. The objective is not to get recalcitrant people to follow orders; it is to invite them to take ownership of a vision, a strategy, a set of values. Dialogue is ideally suited to this objective.

The actual experience of dialogue helps enormously to allay fears of status and power loss. Elites who have had this experience come to realize that they do not relinquish power or status by empowering others to reason together with them as equals. In fact, they gain in authority and respect. The kind of "power" involved in exchanging views in a dialogue setting is not the zero-sum type. In a dialogue, everyone wins. Opening oneself to the views of others through dialogue is an effective way of uniting people to advance shared goals. As we have seen, dialogue mutes conflict, creates a sense of community and goodwill, causes people to react sympathetically to one another as people rather than to negative stereotypes, and nudges people toward the same side of an issue rather than fixing them on opposite sides. In Lyndon Johnson's earthy rationale for including people in the reasoning process leading up to decision making, "It's better to have them inside the tent pissing out than outside pissing in."

In brief, the fear of losing status through inviting the public into decision making is allayed once elites encounter the actual experience of dialogue as part of their effort to shift from command-and-control leadership to relational leadership.

ADDRESSING THE BLIND SPOT

The blind spot—the major obstacle subverting politicians' will—is the elites' conviction that an ill-informed public cannot make any significant contribution to policy because average citizens cannot conceivably possess the knowledge that professionals bring to the table. This is a particularly obdurate obstacle to surmount, in part because the concern is legitimate. There are many occasions when the public really is so bogged down in inconsistent, moralistic, narrowly self-interested, and unrealistic wishful thinking that greater public engagement would make policy decisions worse, not better. Mindful of this reality, most elites feel that resorting to dialogue is a waste of time and energy. I am referring here not to leaders who are elitists or snobs but to those who sincerely believe in democracy and are committed to sounding out their policy proposals with the public. These leaders may be eager to learn how people react to the policy proposals they originate, but they really do not want to hear the public's ideas or to engage the public as equals.

The reluctance is understandable. It is romantic nonsense to assume that people who haven't given a moment's thought to an issue are going to be able to make a constructive contribution to it. And regarding many issues, the public has *not* given them a moment's thought.

Here is where dialogue becomes particularly important. Many mechanisms already exist for giving the public a voice in shaping policies, such as polls, debates, referenda, lobbies, and interest groups. Dialogue does not compete with these mechanisms (e.g., dialogue preceding a public opinion poll or a referendum on an issue would ensure sounder policy). The main reason for resorting to dialogue is that it addresses the legitimate concern of elites that the public is not always prepared to address issues in a thoughtful and considered manner. One of dialogue's great strengths is that it gives people the best possible opportunity to come to grips with issues. In a dialogue setting, the public will be as responsive to the arguments and information that leaders present as leaders are to the public's concerns. Dialogue is a unique method for transforming people's views from raw, mushy, and unrealistic wishful thinking into the kind of thoughtful and considered judgment that should allay the legitimate concerns of elites.

The other source of the elites' blind spot—and it is a far more insidious form of resistance—is a set of deeply rooted but erroneous assumptions built into our culture's dominant model of knowledge. Most officials, managers, and professionals live by the paradigm of knowledge as being information-driven. From this standpoint, the public's inferior level of information (relative to that of experts and professionals) and its tendency to judge issues in terms of moral values introduces random elements of ignorance and subjectivity into what should be an objective, well-informed process.

The assumptions underlying this paradigm are:

1. that policy making requires expert knowledge,
2. that expert knowledge involves specialized factual information, and
3. that the public cannot usefully contribute to policy making because it lacks this specialized information.

These assumptions are so universally shared and so utterly taken for granted that they are rarely examined. For this reason they are held with extraordinary tenacity; they undercut policy makers' motivation to do dialogue with the public far more than reluctance to share power does. After all, talking things over with employees, voters, or fellow citizens is not a serious challenge to a leader's power. But the suspicion that one is wasting one's time and energy in empty ritual will dampen any leader's enthusiasm. It is these assumptions about the knowledge requirements for policy making that give leaders a seemingly rational reason for not doing what they don't want to do anyway, namely, go through the considerable trouble of entering into dialogue with a poorly informed public.

Chapter 12

Dialogue as a Path to Public Judgment

Several years after I started to do public opinion research in the 1950s, my doubts about the indoctrination I had received in my graduate school training began to grow stronger. By the 1970s, I had developed serious reservations about the conventional paradigm of knowledge I had absorbed in the Philosophy and Social Relations Departments at Harvard. I found that my surveys of public opinion raised a number of puzzling questions whose answers took me decades to resolve.

Why, I wondered, is there such extreme variation in the quality of public opinion? On some issues people's opinions express nothing more than their own unrealistic wishful thinking or echo what some TV newsreader said that morning. On other issues, people have deliberated thoughtfully, exchanged views with others, and formed judgments of startling clarity and realism. In conducting public opinion polls, there are times when opinions do come across as steeped in ignorance, misinformation, prejudice, and mindlessness. But there are also times when people's opinions are thoughtful and down to earth, bristling with good sense and wisdom.

Good quality of public opinion does not mean that the public happens to agree with elites or that people have a lot of facts at their fingertips (they rarely do). Good quality means that people don't flip-flop every time they are asked a slightly different question, that they are reasonably consistent in their views and don't contradict themselves every time they voice their opinion, and, above all, that they are fully aware of the consequences of their own views and take responsibility for their opinions.

Extreme variation in the quality of public opinion occurs not only from issue to issue but also on the same issue at different points in time. In the early stages of the development of an issue, people seem oblivious to the consequences of their opinions and their views are mushy and full of contradictions. In later stages, their views grow settled, firm, and thoughtful.

In the course of conducting hundreds of studies of public opinion, I have watched as the public has gradually clarified its thinking on issues of importance to it, and eventually arrived at thoughtful, considered conclusions. I began to think of these as "public judgments." For example, in the 1950s the US public came to the judgment that solitary go-it-alone leadership doesn't make sense for America and that the United States needs allies to help it carry out the leadership responsibilities of a great power. Ever since, the public has never wavered from this judgment, even in periods when foreign affairs distract public attention from urgent domestic concerns or when America's political leadership is tempted to act alone against the wishes of our nation's friends and allies.

In the early 1990s I wrote a book, *Coming to Public Judgment,* in which I described the various stages through which people's thinking about issues evolves as they progress from unenlightened raw opinion to considered judgment.[1] Gradually, I came to realize that the public's moral judgments reflect a form of knowledge and insight that is distinctively different from the more formal types of scientific and professional knowledge that push values aside in the interest of focusing solely on "the facts."

In public judgment, facts and values are indistinguishable from each other. The average person judges whether a policy makes sense without differentiating sharply between practical and moral considerations. In making a judgment, people take into account the facts as they understand them *and* their personal goals and moral values *and* their sense of what is best for others as well as themselves.

For example, in weighing the pros and cons of decriminalizing drugs, people tend to make their judgments on whether "it is the right thing to do" and not only on whether it might reduce crime rates.

The public's anger at managed health care organizations for putting profits ahead of people's health reflects their sense that such policies are destructive both morally and practically.

As we have seen, in arriving at a moral judgment about Social Security people take into account their own financial needs for retirement and those of others they care about, and balance these against their goals, moral values, and what they think is best for the society.

When majorities of the public form judgments about capital punishment, whether for or against, they understand that sometimes the criminal justice system miscarries and innocent people are condemned to death, and simultaneously they take into account their own values about the sacredness of life, the requirements of justice, and the well-being of the society. Their social values and personal morality, their interpretation of the meaning of life, and whatever statistics they happen to know about crime rates are all aspects of a single, indivisible judgment.

We can, of course, separate out the factual information and the values analytically into two piles and insist that policy makers, in the interests of objectivity, put their values aside. But in doing so, we would be playing a game of abstraction that will lead to many undesirable dead ends (such as the proliferation of gun-for-hire lawyers and political spinmeisters who park their ethics at the door in the name of professionalism).

I remember when public opinion turned against the Vietnam War. The elites in Washington, "the best and the brightest," as David Halberstam ironically labeled them, were hung up on their "village pacification ratios" and other quasi facts long after the public had reached its considered judgment that the effort was no longer worth the cost. The public's judgment was essentially a moral one, and it was a form of knowledge superior to the mountain of factual information at the disposal of the leadership in Washington.

It is not that policy makers deride judgment as a human quality. On the contrary, good judgment is highly valued. But it is valued as a personality trait, like being courteous to strangers or having a good sense of humor. It is not seen as a formal requirement for making policy or practicing one's profession. Some people have good judgment; others do not. That's the way the chips fall. In choosing people to fill top-level policy positions, good judgment is sometimes highly valued. But it is not something leaders expect from the public. And when it comes to defining the kind of formal knowledge needed for shaping policy, moral judgment is usually left out of consideration. The assumption is that moral judgment is one thing, knowledge is another; let's not get the two mixed up.

DIALOGUE FOR REACHING PUBLIC JUDGMENT

Another source of puzzlement to me has been the great disparity between the conventional view of how best to improve the quality of public opinion and the actual process of how people go about improving their own opinions. According to the conventional view, good quality of public opinion comes from being well informed; poor quality of public opinion is synonymous with being badly informed.

It would be perverse to deny that in many situations factual information is relevant to quality of opinion. If I want to know whether a bridge is safe to drive on, I want the best-informed expert opinion available. But if I want to know which one of two candidates will make the better president, I would place more trust in the judgment of the voters than in the well-informed views of the TV pundits who follow the campaign.

In a professional lifetime devoted to studying public opinion, I have come to the conclusion that it is a serious blunder to equate sound public opinion with people's having a lot of factual information. Obviously, information plays some role in shaping public opinion. But usually it is a secondary role. To assume that public opinion is invariably improved by inundating people with data greatly exaggerates the relevance and importance of information.[2]

If information plays a secondary role in the process whereby people convert raw, ill-considered, and unstable opinion into thoughtful, realistic judgment, what, then, is primary? Over a period of years, it gradually dawned on me that the creative processes whereby people convert raw opinion into considered judgments are essentially dialogic.

All three essential characteristics of dialogue contribute to improving the quality of public judgment. Empathic listening, for example, is indispensable to forming sound public judgments. The quality of people's opinions improves as they attend to the views and experiences of others. I have watched people's views change on a variety of issues—attitudes toward their employers, immigration, health care, school reform, teenage pregnancy, assisted suicide, race relations, drug abuse, free speech, punishment for crimes, the US president's sex habits—when they have been exposed to a diversity of viewpoints and have listened to them empathically. In forming their own judgments, it is very helpful for people to hear how others feel about the same issues that concern them.

The ability of people to influence one another as equals also contributes to the quality of public opinion. As in all forms of dialogue, the quality of public opinion is best served when coercive pressure is reduced to its barest minimum. An interesting example is the growth of the gender gap in US presidential elections in the 1980s and 1990s. Before that time, the women's vote followed the men's. The disparity between the political outlook of men and women culminated in the huge gender gap of 1996—a whopping 26 percentage points. The huge disparity between the male and female vote reflected the growing autonomy of women as they freed themselves from the pressures of husbands and fathers. (In the 1996 election, men and women of both political parties held strikingly different attitudes toward the role of government in maintaining a social safety net for those in need.)

The dialogic process of laying bare one's most cherished assumptions—the third essential feature of making judgments—works as well as it does because of a dynamic that psychologists call "working through": the hard work involved when people absorb, assimilate, and adapt to emotion-laden events such as failures, separations, and traumas that cause them to question their most cherished assumptions. Factual information free of emotion takes very little time to "work through." A woman writes a note to her husband saying "I am leaving your dinner in the fridge." The husband takes no longer to digest this bit of factual information than he does to read the note. But suppose that instead of the note reading "I am leaving your dinner in the fridge," it read, "I am leaving *you*." The information content is conveyed instantly. But it may take months or years for the husband to work through its full emotional meaning.

REPRESENTATIVE THINKING

Why is the exchange of views in dialogue so much more effective in advancing people's understanding than the more direct forms of conveying information to people in the form of news reports, articles, or books? The writings of the late philosopher Hannah Arendt provide us with an insightful answer. She believes that dialogue is a powerful method for uncovering and testing the truths of human experience. It does so through a process that Arendt calls "representative thinking."

In dialogue, I present my own unique way of looking at an issue. I then heed your way of looking at it. A third and a fourth and a fifth participant in the dialogue present their perspectives. The judgment of all participants is enriched by their ability to incorporate all of the varied perspectives. We are mutually engaged in representative thinking.

When people who share a common purpose do dialogue,

each participant develops a depth of perspective that is not possible when the issue is examined from a single point of view. Through dialogue we fashion a communal perspective on the goals and values that guide our lives. To this search for mutual understanding we bring our entire life experience.

When spoken by an individual, the familiar phrase "It seems to me . . ." is just an idiosyncratic opinion. But as dialogue unfolds and people interact with one another, modifying their points of view, each "It seems to me . . ." is tempered and enriched in the light of others. All of the "It seems to me . . ." judgments add up to something more than a random collection of opinions; they reveal an issue viewed from a great variety of perspectives and experiences: they show representative thinking at work. Such truth seeking is a joint endeavor in which we actively pool our collective wisdom. The truths of how to live together can, Arendt argued, be gained only by representing reality from this kind of variety of perspectives.

For this understanding to develop and grow, the shared problems and values of those who would form a community must be viewed from many different perspectives. Out of this cauldron of communal consideration a limited number of shared understandings will be formed, some of which will prove to be transitory while others will stand the test of time.

Thus, in helping people to move from raw opinion to considered judgment, dialogue engages them in a complex, time-consuming, intensely involving process as they agonize over how to take the perspectives of others into account as they match the facts with their values and feelings on troubling issues.

This process is sharply different from elites' decision making, in which a conscious effort is made to push values into the background in the interest of preserving objectivity. But life being what it is, the values that are shoved out the front door sneak in through the back door. Values can never be excluded from policy decisions. When we try to do so, we delude ourselves.

Chapter 13

From Expert Knowledge to Wisdom

My first full-time job was with a business research firm in New York in the early 1950s. The firm immediately assigned me to a research project for a client, the Burroughs Adding Machine Company of Detroit, Michigan.[1] As the project progressed, I grew more and more enthusiastic about our work because it brought to light information important to the company's future. When the head of the firm, a thoughtful and perceptive man named Roger Nowland, failed to send the final report to the company as soon as it was finished, I felt keenly disappointed.

After a week had passed with the report still undelivered, I asked Mr. Nowland when he intended to mail it to the client. "You can't send a report like that in the mail," he said with some annoyance. It raises all sorts of questions about the way the company does its business and it calls on them to make big changes. We'll have to go to Detroit and present it in person. That's what I'm trying to arrange."

I remember arguing with him: "Isn't it a waste of time and money for us to take a sleeper back and forth to Detroit?" (There were no jets at the time.) "Besides," I added, "there isn't much we can add to what is already in the report. Isn't it better for them to read it at their own pace than to have to listen to so many detailed findings in one sitting?"

He replied, "Oh boy, have you got a lot to learn!" Patiently, he explained the facts of life to me: "There's a lot at stake for them. If they do what the report suggests, it's going to cost them millions of dollars. And it's a huge risk. Top executives don't make up their minds from a piece of paper. Our fancy methodology isn't going to convince them. They want to see us, ask us questions, see if we know what we're talking about. They trust me because I've been working with them for years. But this is a bigger deal than anything I've done for them up to now. And the only thing they know about you is that you're young and inexperienced. Luckily, they don't know what an innocent you are. They have to size you up, see if you speak with forked tongue."

I respected Mr. Nowland's judgment. But I still thought it odd that a company would spend tens of thousands of dollars on a factual inquiry conducted in the most rigorous fashion and then judge its validity through an oral presentation and a conversation with us. It didn't make sense to me. I had come from the world of academic standards. I wasn't familiar with the practical world.

That was my first exposure to two different ways of assessing validity—through formal methodologies and through making practical judgments about the people doing the research. In subsequent years, I would recall my youthful naïveté with embarrassment. It soon became apparent to me that there was *always* a gap between facts and the decisions executives make, and the more important the decision, the larger the gap. To cope, executives learn to place their confidence in a combination of their own experience, available information (however limited), and their personal values applied to judging people.

Overcoming the Fact/Value Split

Most policies depend far more on values than on factual information. In our political system, for policies to be acceptable they must be seen as consonant with a wide range of values such as fairness, freedom, compassion, safety, moral legitimacy, the preservation of public order, and so on. In policies that arouse the most passion and concern, these values often conflict with each other. Current drug policy, for example, insists that marijuana be branded as an illegal substance, even though from a pragmatic point of view decriminalizing pot might reduce crime rates. Here the value of public safety conflicts with the value of moral legitimacy. Proposals for education reform to give vouchers to parents so that they can select the school of their choice for their children pit the value of preserving the public school system against the value of individual choice. Welfare reform that requires mothers of young children to enter the workforce even though doing so may not be good for the children pits fairness against concern for children.

All significant social policies call for weighing competing values against one another and playing them off against whatever factual information may be available. In this complex process, the interaction among people creates shared perspectives in which facts and values are inextricably intertwined. These shared perspectives, in which values are central, constitute an important form of knowledge. It is not fake knowledge, second-rate knowledge, or mere ventilation of feelings. It is simply a different kind of knowledge than the kind experts generate. In our culture, however, value-laden perspectives aren't considered to be knowledge and so are not taken seriously when policy is being shaped.

Why don't they count as knowledge?

This troublesome question brings us face-to-face with our society's most entrenched paradigm of knowledge. This paradigm sharply divides facts from values. Facts belong in the world of knowledge; values belong in the world of feelings and preferences that have nothing to do with knowledge.

In philosophy, this assumption is sometimes called the "theory of emotivism," which British philosopher Alasdair MacIntyre defines as follows:

> Emotivism is the doctrine that all evaluative judgments, and more specifically, all moral judgments are *nothing but* expressions of preference, expressions of attitudes or feeling, insofar as they are moral or evaluative in character.[2]

The leaders of our institutions are far more steeped than the public in this paradigm. Indeed, the sharp dichotomy between values and facts is an important part of our elites' intellectual heritage and professional competence. Facts are automatically categorized as knowledge, and values are categorized as feelings, beliefs, and convictions that get in the way of knowledge.

Leaders know how much discipline it takes to stay with the facts and not let their own wishful thinking and personal values confuse issues. They perceive, correctly, that the public does not observe this discipline and that the average person is long on feelings and opinions and short on factual information. In their view, to enter into dialogue with the public for purposes of shaping policy is to put feelings ahead of facts and to compromise the standards associated with objectivity, professionalism, expertise, and specialization. In effect, to endorse dialogue with the public enthusiastically, they would have to abandon a paradigm of knowledge that is as much a part of them as the way they sign their name or part their hair.

Even leaders who are flexible about most things will cling tenaciously to the cognitive frameworks they developed in their youth for coping with the confusion of the world. These tend to be among the deepest layers of one's buried assumptions. They are difficult to change even when they have grown obsolete and dysfunctional.

In the fact/value split, some readers will recognize the influence of a school of thought known as "logical positivism," which reached its peak of influence in the middle years of the twentieth century. The positivist paradigm of knowledge makes a particularly sharp distinction between empirically grounded scientific knowledge, which it regards as the only valid form of knowledge, and the unscientific world of opinions, values, feelings, and beliefs that most of us inhabit most of the time.

Though the influence of logical positivism has waned in the academic world, it remains strong in the general culture. Indeed, it is difficult to exaggerate how pervasive it still is, how much influence it has on our culture even today, and how much resistance it generates to the kinds of claims I am making (i.e., that by blending facts and values together, dialogue can create valid knowledge, though not the kind that science recognizes as knowledge).

Philosopher Richard Bernstein argues that we must find a way to escape the false alternatives with which traditional philosophy has saddled us: a value-free world of "facts" with its conception of knowledge as "a correct representation of what is objective" and a nihilistic relativism in which all moral decisions are reduced to idiosyncratic preferences, thereby stripping them of validity. In his book *The New*

Constellation, Bernstein cites dialogue as a way of testing goals and values.[3]

The influence of the fact/value dichotomy has had enormous consequences for our civilization, both good and bad. The split gives rise to a mentality that makes it easy to find technical fixes for problems but difficult to find solid grounds for goals and ultimate values. As a result we are becoming technological giants and sociological midgets. At an accelerating pace, we produce a mind-boggling flow of technological marvels at the same time as our civic virtues of mutual respect, trust, concern, neighborliness, community, love, and caring are slowly eroding. It has become a platitude to observe that human wisdom has failed to keep pace with technological prowess. But rarely do we reflect on why this is so and what can be done about it.

It is so, at least partly, because our culture is hooked on splitting the world into artificially separate compartments of facts and values. The solution is to become less rigid about the split and to devote more attention to ways of knowing, including dialogue, that intermingle values and facts.

Webster defines wisdom as "the ability to judge soundly and to deal sagaciously with the facts, especially as they relate to life and conduct." This dictionary definition helps us to distinguish between information and wisdom. Information is fact-driven. Wisdom is the more encompassing term; it goes beyond factual knowledge by adding values to facts. Since most public policies bear on life and conduct, we need to bring values as well as factual knowledge to bear. The methods of science and professional expertise are excellent for generating factually based knowledge; the methods of dialogue are excellent for dealing with this knowledge wisely. The point of engaging the public in dialogue is that by adding the value-rich perspectives of the public to the information-rich perspectives of the expert, we can create wiser policies.

Microlending

The evolution of a form of banking known as "microlending" gives us a vivid example of policies that in mixing factual knowledge and moral values together create wise social innovation. Microlending was the invention of a charismatic banker, Muhammad Yunus, head of the Grameen Bank of Bangladesh. His story is well known. He started giving tiny loans out of his own pocket to women in his village. He said that his first loan was for five cents to a woman who worked for two cents a day because she could not afford the five cents needed to buy the bamboo to make her own baskets. Shortly thereafter, his bank started to make small loans (some for as little as twenty dollars) to women in the village to provide them with capital to buy supplies for weaving cloth. He found that the women were scrupulous in paying back the loans (more scrupulous, in fact, than well-heeled customers), even though they had no collateral to cover their loans in the event of default.

Yunus had discovered a method for addressing one of the most serious problems of world poverty: poor people's lack of access to capital. His example inspired others in various parts of the world to pursue comparable microlending programs. The biggest microlending program in the industrialized world is now in Poland. A remarkable young banker, Rosalind Copisarov, manages it for the Polish-American Bank. The bank makes small loans to people in Poland who would not ordinarily qualify for bank credit.

Several years ago Poland was struck by one of the worst floods of the century, affecting hundreds of thousands of people. The World Bank, the U.S. government, and other governments immediately announced that they would make disaster relief money available. But months later, not a penny had been dispensed. The reason was the difficulty these institutions had in arriving at factually objective criteria for allocating the relief money. For all practical purposes, the vast resources of the World Bank and a variety of governments were rendered impotent in providing aid to Poland's flood victims in a timely fashion because their insistence on objective, factually grounded criteria blinded them to the claims of other values.

Recognizing the urgency of people's needs, Ms. Copisarov was able to secure extra funding to provide immediate help to flood victims. Because recipients would need easier repayment terms (having been flooded out of their homes and businesses), she entered into dialogue with potential recipients, and together they shaped a lending program that met the bank's needs for eventual repayment as well as the urgent needs of the victims.

Loan recipients were organized into groups of five families. Each family decided on the amount of damage and the size of the loan the other families in the group would receive. As one dialogue participant wittily observed, "No Pole would ever permit another Pole to get more than he deserved." The bank eased the terms of repayment but in all other ways treated the relief money as loans that the recipients were obliged to repay. The bank also followed other policies that had emerged from the dialogue between bank staff members and flood victims.

Rosalind Copisarov brings true wisdom to her job. Wisdom is reflected in the bank's mission statement and in the amount of discretion and judgment given to individual loan officers. Wisdom is reflected in the bank's insistence on building relationships of trust between loan officers and borrowers, trust that is indispensable to the successful functioning of the program. And there is wisdom in the blend of profit objectives and compassion that the bank brings to its microlending program. The very concept of microlending shows how inseparable values and facts are in the shaping of policy.

The claim that policy should be grounded in judgments that mix fact and value together collides so directly with the positivist paradigm of knowledge that either the claim must be false or the paradigm flawed. Since I believe that the claim is valid, the fault must lie with the paradigm.

It is here that controversy arises. My goal is not to propose some grand new paradigm of knowledge in order to justify a claim about the truth value of dialogue; that would be like building a library in order to house one book. Far more modestly, I am proposing to take a single step outside the conventional paradigm by challenging the usefulness of the rigid distinction between facts and values when it comes to discovering truths about human living.

As a method of adding wisdom to knowledge, dialogue ought to enjoy greater credibility than it now has. Without such credibility it will remain a mere nicety, suitable for earnest civic groups practicing citizenship or for organizations seeking to build closer bonds among people who work together. With it, it will become a powerful tool both for shaping policy and for strengthening our democracy.

A PLETHORA OF WAYS OF KNOWING

The roots of the elites' blind spot run even deeper than entrapment in the rigidities of the fact/value dichotomy. They go all the way back to the very foundations of our civilization. In Western culture it has always been difficult to sustain the self-evident truth that there are many different ways of knowing, each with its own special strengths and drawbacks. It may seem like ordinary common sense to assume that there are all sorts of ways of knowing and that one particular way (factual knowledge) should not be elevated above all others. But this perspective doesn't take history into account. One of our deepest historical traditions is the assumption that knowledge comes in the form of a hierarchy.

I recall my first encounter with this concept as a college student. Our philosophy professor introduced us to the Platonic allegory of the cave in which masses of common people sit huddled together staring at shadows cast on a wall without understanding that the shadows themselves are not actual objects but rather mere tricks of light.

Plato believed that only the philosophically trained few can grasp the true nature of reality in the form of immutable and universal Ideas. For Plato, these Ideas occupy the summit of the hierarchy of knowledge, while at the bottom are the shadows in the cave. The many ignorant souls crammed into the cave mistake these shadows for reality.

Astonishingly, the idea of knowledge as a hierarchy has persisted for 2,500 years, although the form of knowledge privileged to perch at the very top has changed a number of times. Over the centuries the Platonic Ideas were displaced from their privileged position at the apex of the hierarchy by other contenders for top billing such as conceptions of God revealed through faith, conceptions of reason revealed through logic, and, ever since Newtonian physics in the seventeenth century, the laws of nature revealed through scientific inquiry.

But the bottom spot on the hierarchy has never changed. There, occupying the pits, never being elevated above their lowly rank, are found the judgments of the masses, still deemed to be imprisoned in a dark cave of ignorance and prejudice, mistaking appearances for reality.

To myself and others privileged to attend elite colleges, it made perfect sense that we were being trained as an intellectual and professional elite who would be privy to the highest reaches of knowledge, separating us from and elevating us above the opinions of the mass of people, who do not have access to the same knowledge. In earlier eras, priests who had been trained to believe that their form of sacred knowledge belonged at the top of the hierarchy must have felt the same thrill at being initiated into the mysteries of true knowledge. Many of today's elites share this same conviction that they possess a higher order of knowledge than others in the society.

Like most people raised in the Western tradition, I began my professional life with the assumption that knowledge is ordered in a hierarchical fashion, with science at the top, professional and scholarly knowledge in the middle, and the opinions of the mass public at the bottom. It did not take long for disillusionment to set in. After several years of studying the opinions of the public, I realized with a shock that the average person possessed insights different from, but certainly not inferior to, the knowledge of elites. Yet for most of my professional life I was rarely able to convince those who had little contact with the public of the validity of this insight. They were too immersed in the tradition of the hierarchy to see what, from their point of view, had to be a disagreeable reality they would rather not see.

Fortunately, as the new millennium opens before us, the tradition of a hierarchy of knowledge has begun to weaken. It has been so deeply ingrained in Western culture that this is an event of moment. One of the most significant shifts in our era's Zeitgeist is the gradual emergence of pluralistic ways of knowing.

The attack on the view of knowledge as a single hierarchy

with science in the top spot has been led by scholars in the humanistic tradition such as philosopher Richard Rorty, who argues that knowledge is more a "matter of acquiring habits of action for coping with reality" than it is "a matter of getting reality right."[4] As a pragmatist, he conceives of knowledge as providing us with a tool kit for coping with the world, with each tool having its own purposes and capabilities. You don't use a buzz saw to screw in a screw, you use a screwdriver. But unlike the positivists, you don't make the foolish claim that a buzz saw is a tool and a screwdriver is not.

Each tool of knowledge has its own appropriate uses, those of science being to understand, predict, and control nature while those of dialogue and related ways of knowing are designed to understand the human predicament and the truths of living. Rorty conceives of these various tools as instruments for continually reweaving the web of ideas and beliefs that guide our lives and our actions. The ideas that come from science and the ideas that come from dialogue are both parts of the web of knowledge.[5]

Another influential philosopher, Jürgen Habermas, has devoted a large part of his life's work to elaborating a theory of pluralistic ways of knowing. Habermas has tirelessly argued that knowledge is *inextricably* linked to human purpose and is never a stand-alone body of information and theories. This means that instead of a single hierarchy of knowledge there are multiple ways of knowing, each appropriate for a different purpose.

Knowledge, then, is a pluralistic phenomenon. For purposes of gaining control over people and things, the knowledge of technical and scientific experts has proven superior to other ways of knowing. But for the truths of human experience—learning how to live together in peaceful, creative, civilized societies—technical expert knowledge is awkward, heavy-handed, and unresponsive. It fails to address the great questions of how to live, what values to pursue, what meaning to find in life, how to achieve a just and humane world, and how to be a fully realized human person—all essentially issues of judgment often arrived at through dialogue.

In the larger society as well as in philosophical circles, the idea of hierarchy is weakening, replaced by concepts of pluralism. The work of Howard Gardner and others[6] has shown that there are multiple forms of intelligence, not a single hierarchy that can be measured through IQ tests. Even in the field of health care, where scientific knowledge enjoys great prestige, some elbowroom is being made for alternative medicine. The mainstream medical profession remains skeptical toward practices such as acupuncture, and most physicians want to evaluate alternative medicine by familiar scientific standards. Yet ever so tentatively, some parts of the medical profession are becoming more open-minded about forms of alternative medicine that do not fit its model of science.

The line of thought that has been developing over these past few decades adds up to this: we ought to discard onto the scrap heap of history the assumption of a single hierarchy of knowledge. The theoretical justification for excluding the public from policy formation is based on a narrow hierarchical conception of knowledge that excludes the wisdom of the collectivity—arguably, the most indispensable virtue of sound policy. Instead of levels of knowledge within a hierarchy, we ought to visualize a variety of ways of knowing, each designed to meet a different purpose, each with its own ground rules and its own excellences and limitations. The kinds of truths that dialogue reveals are not the truths of scientific and technical expertise. They belong to a different order of knowing—the domain of human wisdom.

The appeal to do more dialogue presented in earlier parts of this book has been relatively free of controversy. There are few serious objections to the "feel-good" benefits of dialogue, namely, that those engaged in it come to share a common bond with other participants, that it helps to clarify people's thinking, and that it is good for democracy for citizens to talk things over among themselves and with their leaders. Leaders are also aware of dialogue's public relations benefits in that it gives their followers a feeling of empowerment and participation, while it gives the leaders themselves valuable feedback.

Where my thesis becomes controversial is in its added claim that dialogue-based public judgments blending facts and moral values (the product of dialogue) are a legitimate form of knowledge that contributes practicality and wisdom—as valuable for the kinds of truths it seeks as science is for its kinds of truths.

It would be nonsense to claim that dialogue gives answers to life's dilemmas and that through dialogue people will find values to live by. The knowledge claims I am making for dialogue are much more modest. We need to use dialogue to focus on the collective problems of living together in communities. For all of its powers, scientific expertise has no answers for us here. But dialogue can help us discover the truths of living together *if* we change the prevailing paradigm of truth and wisdom.

In summary, the strategy I am proposing in this part of the book is aimed at reducing elite resistance by focusing on the obsolete nature of the fact/value dichotomy and the notion of a single hierarchy of knowledge—the main intellectual supports of the elites' blind spot. To be credible, it is necessary to acknowledge from the outset the legitimate concern of elites that a compulsive and automatic resort to public engagement is a terrible idea. The last thing we want to do is to bog policy makers down in an overly idealistic or naively populist conception that "the people" are always ahead of the experts and elites. Going this route would rob the concept of public engagement of its seriousness.

Having made this acknowledgment, however, the next step in the argument is to deconstruct the elites' blind spot. It makes no sense to draw sharp lines between facts and values or to assume that there is one and only one path to knowledge and truth. I believe that the judicious use of dialogue can transform the public into an invaluable partner of leaders and elites in shaping policy because dialogue brings forth the wisdom inherent in the collective public experience.

Chapter 14

The Struggle for the Soul

Up to this point I have focused on the uses of public dialogue to resolve policy issues such as health care, Social Security, and school reform. But dialogue's most valuable contribution to the society is likely to come in relation to more general concerns about what kind of civilization the West will become in the future.

Dialogue serves best when we as a people are confronted with equally legitimate but one-sided visions of the future and asked to choose between them. If they are truly one-sided, being forced to make a choice leads to a dead end. Sustained, hardheaded dialogue can help us avoid making that false choice and forge a new vision that transcends the limits of each.

We now finds ourselves in the early stages of precisely this kind of struggle for the soul. The nature of the struggle is not yet self-evident because so much of it is taking place beneath the surface. It is a struggle between two one-sided visions of our future: the Vision of the Free Market and the Vision of Civil Society.

Underlying the first vision is the conviction that in the new global economy, the free market, driven by technology and entrepreneurship, will shape a more prosperous, democratic, and secure world than we have ever known before. The conviction supporting the second is that to renew our society and halt its moral decline we must return to the noble—and profoundly traditional—dream of societies past. In practice, this means finding a way to strengthen the values of community, faith, responsibility, civic virtue, neighborliness, stewardship, and mutual concern for each other, values that are not inherent in a free-market economy.

These distinct visions, each with its own mix of the positive and the negative, are engaged with each other in epic combat. In what follows, I present a brief sketch of each one and explain why I believe the stakes are so high as to warrant characterizing their encounter as a struggle for the soul, and why dialogue can play a critically important role in resolving the struggle.

THE VISION OF THE FREE MARKET

"The Long Boom," an article that appeared in *Wired* magazine in the late 1990s, presented a highly idealized expression of the Vision of the Free Market.[1] It conjured up the vision of a United States–led sustained economic boom of twenty-five years' duration destined to usher in a new golden age of freedom and prosperity for the entire globe—eradicating poverty, stimulating social mobility, reducing crime and violence, reviving family values, easing ethnic rivalries, educating the unskilled, and "forming a new civilization, a global civilization, distinct from those that arose on the planet before."[2]

Despite its utopian tone, the article captures the strand of optimistic idealism that often underlies the gruffest of bottom-line voices. Many of the world's leading business executives and political leaders believe that the free market has moral virtues over and above its pragmatic advantages in allocating resources efficiently. It is these moral virtues that give the Vision of the Free Market its ideological and political power.

The most probable scenario for the near future is that some form of this free-market vision will prevail. At the moment, it dominates the American climate of opinion. Indeed, so robust is its dynamism that the media refer to America's enthusiastic embrace of free-market economic philosophy as "triumphalism"—a joyous shout to the rest of the world that the American economic system has, once again, proven its superiority over all others.

Eventually, the air of heady triumphalism will pass. But there is little doubt that American technology–driven high-entrepreneurship market economy is the model for the rest of the world and is destined to shape people's lives for decades, if not centuries, to come.

No one should minimize the appeal of this vision to the American people or its importance in making the promise of the American Dream a reality. The prospect of greater material well-being serves a purpose that goes far beyond materialism: it helps to validate the American Dream. As historians such as David Potter have pointed out, Americans are a people of plenty.[3] Material well-being is indispensable to a system of upward mobility. The American Dream depends on an economy that can deliver rewards for hard work and self-improvement.

But the Vision of the Free Market has its dark side. Many of those who endow market capitalism with almost magical powers are well aware of it but accept it as the price of progress. The late economist Joseph Schumpeter, a strong supporter of free-market capitalism, underscored capitalism's power of "creative destruction," its tendency to act as an uncontrollable force of nature: impersonal, implacable, and in the short run radically disruptive of jobs, skills, and older enterprises. For those who succeed in riding the back of the tiger, the capitalism of the free market is wonderful. But it holds less appeal for those who fall in the path of its creative destruction. As we have seen recently in Asia, adherence to an untrammeled market economy can bring great suffering and disaster in its wake.

The Luddites of nineteenth-century Britain who smashed factory machines were not opposed to new machines in principle. Indeed, they would have welcomed them if they had saved or enhanced their jobs. They lashed out against them because they cost them their livelihood.

We have fewer Luddites today because technology is rightfully seen as bringing us far greater benefits than costs. Thanks in part to technology, the free market creates far more winners than it did in the past. But it also creates many more losers—a nasty reality that those who preach the Vision of the Free Market gloss over. Over the past few decades the incomes of those in the bottom quintile of the population have declined seriously, and if the education system doesn't soon improve, the long-term prospects for the majority of the workforce who lack a college degree or high-wage technical skills will be bleak.

In addition to these familiar negatives, the market economy has a more subtle drawback. Those who subscribe to the Vision of the Free Market attribute moral virtues to the market that it does not, in fact, possess. If one reads between the lines, free-market advocates never depend solely on the market mechanism for their optimistic scenarios of the future. Invariably, they sneak values into the mix that have their source in parts of the culture unrelated to market economics.

Visionaries of the free market stress individualism, freedom, democracy, choice, flexibility, creativity, openness, adaptability to change, self-improvement, self-discipline, leadership, and responsibility. Somehow they assume that these moral virtues are inherent in the practices of a free market. But I believe this is a fallacy. The great economic philosophers of the past, such as Adam Smith (who first enunciated the free-market vision), Thorstein Veblen, and Max Weber, all knew that economic mechanisms cannot sustain a society spiritually. Economic ideas always come embedded in a matrix of social values. The long-term success of the economy as well as the well-being of the larger society depends utterly on these values. But the values themselves do not come from the market economy, and they are not self-sustaining. They need constant reinforcement. If they don't get it from some source other than the market, they wither and die.

It is this false assumption that makes the Vision of the Free Market vulnerable and incomplete. The harsh reality is that the free market is *not* endowed with these moral virtues. In the end, the market is just a practical mechanism for allocating resources. Some individuals, companies, and governments that wield market power use this mechanism wisely and compassionately. Others use their raw economic power mindlessly and couldn't care less about its human consequences. The free market as practiced in China or Thailand or Russia or, in the US, by Ivan Boesky or "Chainsaw Al" Dunlop is not the same free market as practiced by enlightened and morally responsible companies.

Whatever its drawbacks, the free-market vision contains an important truth indispensable to the West's future. The late economist Arthur Okun summed it up well in his formula "The market has a place; the market *in* its place."[4] In the half century following World War II, the mixed economies of the industrialized democracies embodied Okun's formula. They acknowledged that the market has an important place in a free society, but they were determined to contain the "creative destruction" of markets. They assigned a huge role to government in regulating their economies and in supporting a welfare safety net for those unable to be self-sufficient under the conditions of a free market. For a variety of reasons, the mixed economies of the postwar era have lost their credibility. Government is no longer trusted as it once was to keep market forces contained and to soften their creative destructiveness. We are destined to improvise until a new social contract comes along that is capable of achieving this goal.

CIVIL SOCIETY AS A COUNTERVISION

The Vision of Civil Society arises from different sources. Since the late 1980s, in meetings and conferences throughout the nation, leaders from the worlds of politics, religion, local communities, foundations, and universities have engaged in a lively conversation on how to renew the bonds of civil society. The conversation is just beginning to clarify what is meant by civil society, how we can strengthen it, and how in doing so we can confront the threat to our nation's social morality.

US Presidential candidate Bill Bradley offers a useful definition of civil society. He defines civil society as the realm of family, friends, neighbors, schools, churches, and workplaces, and the home of an ethic different from either the self-interest of the market economy or the coercive force of government. He sees the ethic of civil society as reflecting voluntary ties of obligation and embodying values such as reciprocity, respect, trust, stability, neighborliness, civic involvement, and love.

He believes our politicians present false alternatives to voters, forcing us to choose the government *or* the market. Political conservatives offer market solutions to our problems; political liberals fall back on government solutions. For Bradley, these alternatives are misguided; he feels that if our most important problems belong in the domain of civil society, arguing about whether the market or the government should address them misses the point.

Bradley argues that our civilization must rest on a three-legged stool (government, the market economy, *and* civil society). He believes that our political system has neglected the civil society leg of the stool in favor of the other two legs, creating an inherent instability.

In effect, the leaders of the civil society movement are busy shaping a *countervision,* not only to the Vision of the Free Market but to the long-dominant progovernment liberal ideology as well. They see the threat to our society coming from the encroachments of government as well as from the abuses of our market economy. They are mistrustful both of the traditional liberal vision of government as the sole protector of the welfare state and regulator of the market and of the impersonal workings of a market economy. Political scientist Benjamin Barber expresses his fear that our civil society is being squeezed out of existence by the combined forces of "an excessive, elephantine, and paternalistic government and a radically self-absorbed, nearly anarchic private market."[5]

Many advocates of civil society also view with alarm the prevailing version of individualism in our popular culture. They fear that it accentuates the egoistic, short-term, and narcissistic aspects of self, rather than the long-term altruistic aspects. In their view, the preoccupation of baby boomers with "me," "my needs," and "my rights" has inevitably weakened social bonds, social trust, and moral norms.

This form of individualism is, of course, relatively new to

our culture; it came to full expression in the period from the late 1960s to the early 1990s. An earlier ethic also focused on individualism but explicitly linked the individual to the larger society. We are all familiar with the traditional value of "enlightened self-interest," the idea that in serving their own interests, farsighted individuals also contribute to the interests of the larger community. In contrast, the new individualism (in other work I have labeled it "expressive individualism") often takes the form of *unenlightened* self-interest, in pursuit of selfish goals that serve no larger societal interest.

In the ethic of expressive individualism, self-fulfillment comes ahead of responsibility to others, self-expression is valued for its own sake, self-sacrifice is deemed unnecessary— even foolish—and individual choice takes priority over the social taboos that constrain individual desire. The appeal of the expressive life glows far more brightly than the bonds of reciprocal obligations implicit in the traditional values of the past.

Several years ago, the Harvard Business School invited me to conduct a study of its alumni who had graduated long ago, in the post–World War II class of 1949. The class had produced a great many successful executives and entrepreneurs, and the business school was interested in the factors that had contributed to their success, as seen from their own perspective. In my interviews with them, the alumni, mostly retired or semiretired, welcomed the opportunity to reflect back on their lives and the influences on their careers.

What impressed me in their accounts of their business experience was the importance they gave to two factors: luck and parental influence. The most successful ones freely acknowledged the role of luck—being at the right place at the right time, that is, at the outset of the great economic boom that the consumer demand pent up by the war created. But even more important than luck, almost without exception they stressed the values their parents had inculcated in them. Responsibility. Hard work. Family stability. Achievement. Self-discipline. Practicality. Education. Love of country. High moral standards. (Even those who confessed to having cut corners and made compromises cited the moral standards their parents had taught them, from which they had deviated to their own present regret.) In accounting for their success, they were convinced that the technical business skills they had acquired were secondary in importance to these moral values. None mentioned the business school as the source of moral values.

These aging World War II veterans may, of course, be deceiving themselves; a critical observer might account for their success differently. But my own experience in the business world (in a variety of roles, as employee, employer, entrepreneur, consultant, and corporate board member) supports their insight that the moral values they as managers brought to their task were more important than their operating skills. These values did not come from their businesses. They brought the values with them from the larger culture—the influence of parents, schools, friends, the community, the media, the civil society in which they were brought up.

Rereading these interviews, they seem to come from an earlier epoch of American life. There is something quite old-fashioned and out of touch about the role the moral values of their era played in their lives and careers. And because of that, one senses the loss in civil society we are currently feeling.

If the utopianism of the Vision of the Free Market points toward an idealized future, that of the Vision of Civil Society points toward an idealized past. Most leaders of the civil society movement are searching to recover something they believe society once had and now has lost. They hearken back to Alexis de Tocqueville's classic study of American democracy in the early part of the nineteenth century. For de Tocqueville the most remarkable feature of the United States as it then existed was the richness and vitality of its civil society, by which he meant the proliferation of civic groups, community leaders, and voluntary organizations (firefighters, charities, and so on). Through the principle of "association," he pointed out that these voluntary associations assumed a civic responsibility for the well-being of the society absent in the Europe of the time.

Leaders of the civil society movement emphasize the importance of rebuilding a country's "social capital"[6] (the total of the goodwill, volunteer engagement, social activity, and civic virtue of citizens) and of restoring the old balance between rights and responsibilities.[7]

Some (though not all) leaders of the civil society movement romanticize the idea and ideal of community as a place where people automatically belong, where stable extended families live side by side as neighbors who cherish one another and come to one another's aid in times of crisis, a familiar and comfortable place in which to bring up children, develop roots, and practice civic virtue.

Phrases such as "civic virtue" have an old-fashioned ring, and this is deliberate. An essential feature of this countervision is the restoration of traditional values, not only because the alternative is moral decay but also because we cannot otherwise escape the mediocrity, emptiness, and meaninglessness of a society obsessed with mere self-satisfaction and tottering on two legs of a three-legged stool.

The Vision of Civil Society also has a dark side inherent in its close link to the idea of community. In today's societies, the connotations of community are all warm and fuzzy. But historically, tight community bonds have also been associated with narrowness, bigotry, mistrust of outsiders, prying eyes, and stultifying social conformity. Many Germans, for example, are suspicious of such American-based civil society movements as communitarianism because they stir up memories of how the Nazis exploited the emotions linked with the idea of community. In the United States, there are radical groups whose conceptions of community threaten the individual freedoms and choices we most cherish.

A FATEFUL STRUGGLE

When I say that these two visions are engaged in a struggle for the soul, I do not mean that the struggle is one between good and evil in which we must be cheerleaders for the good side and implacable foes of the evil one. The struggle is far more ambiguous. Indeed, our worst fate might be for one of the two visions to so overwhelm the other that it disappears without a trace. Rather, the struggle is between two radically incomplete visions, each of which highlights a desirable aspect of the good society but also builds a false utopia out of this single feature.

I have characterized their encounter as a struggle for the soul. Why such melodramatic language? Why is this encounter different from the many other conflicts of ideas in our long history? Certainly, there is nothing unusual about a swirl of conflicting ideas. Indeed, in many ways the two visions are far less divisive and passionate than the issues that tore the country apart during the Civil War or those that divided the nation in the 1930s or the 1960s. Yet I believe the struggle is

212 THE MAGIC OF DIALOGUE

fateful for our civilization because the two visions so desperately need each other, because for one to triumph over the other would take us down a wrong track from which we might not recover, and because the right sort of synthesis between them has the potential to lift our civilization to new heights of creativity and individual fulfillment.

THE FUTURE OF DIALOGUE

We must develop a larger vision than either the Vision of the Free Market or the Vision of Civil Society, or we will risk losing something indispensable to our spirit. Inevitably, that larger vision must draw sustenance from the past as well as from our future economic prospects, however glorious they may be.

Our destiny must be grounded in a moral vision. The free market by itself cannot sustain this moral vision; values that come from some other source must sustain it.

The Vision of Civil Society is a major source of the moral values that must contain and support the thrust of our market economy. But it limps along far behind the Vision of the Free Market in vitality, enthusiasm, and power. The only reason the Vision of Civil Society has a fighting chance to influence the future is the intensity of the human yearning for the values it symbolizes, such as community, civility, and spirituality. These values are not inherent in a free market economy and are in some ways antagonistic to it.

In a market economy, the function of a business is to offer products and services of good value for a profit. From this purely functional point of view, a business can exist for a very long time at a mediocre level without embracing the

values of civil society—without showing respect for its
employees or customers, without inspiring people to give
their creative best to their jobs, without employees and
management understanding each other, and without employees buying into management's vision of the future (if it
has one). So can our other institutions, such as government
agencies, schools, colleges, foundations, law firms, and
libraries.

But businesses and other organizations are not just economic institutions. They also include people who work side
by side every day and who share common interests and a
common fate that is dependent on how well the organization functions. In this respect a business is also a community, as is a school, a church, a symphony orchestra, a
magazine, a hospital, a branch of science. All of our organizations and institutions have two different roles to play: at
one and the same time, they serve a practical purpose, but
they are also expressions of community and civil society. If
they sacrifice the second role, they inevitably slip into mediocrity or worse.

In serving their practical functions, these organizations can
to some degree exist in isolation from one another. But as
parts of a community and a civil society made up of many
communities, they cannot exist as isolated fragments. They
must communicate with one another, understand one another, trust one another, identify with one another. And to do
all that they cannot rely exclusively on the values of the marketplace or the entitlements and legalisms associated with big
government.

The Vision of the Free Market is a powerful ideology. If it
comes to monopolize our culture, it will inexorably undermine the values of civil society. Concepts such as profit maxi-

mization, short-term profitability, reliance on part-time temporary workers, shareholder value, and downsizing, as well as the accelerating tempo of competition and the ever-widening gap between well-educated, well-paid elites and the majority of citizens will prevail. Ultimately, Oscar Wilde's description of the cynic who "knows the price of everything and the value of nothing" will come to describe our market-driven culture.

On the other hand, we cannot transform our society into a model of civic virtue overnight. Our individualism is too deeply ingrained for us suddenly to become fully civic-minded. We probably never were as virtuous civically as our nostalgia for an earlier society might suggest. As a practical matter, there is no chance that in the struggle between the two visions, the Vision of Civil Society will prevail over the dynamism of the free-market vision. Nor do we want it to do so. Certainly, there are advocates of civil society in our various subcultures (e.g., the academy, the media, our religious institutions) who want this to happen. But pragmatically, it is not going to, nor do the vast majority of the public want it to.

What the majority of the population do want is to "civilize" our market economy: to curb its destructive consequences, to find a way to balance enterprise with the spirit of community, and to realize our deepest spiritual values.

Dialogue can perform this function in two ways, one indirect, the other direct. As an indirect influence, the very process of dialogue has a "civilizing" influence. Dialogue binds us together as communities. To engage in genuine dialogue is to create and strengthen such values of civil society as:

- Building trust in one another
- Feeling familiar and comfortable together
- Finding it easy and natural to cooperate with one another and knowing how to create the common ground on which successful cooperation depends
- Weaving a complex web of working relationships that cut across institutional boundaries (e.g., sanitation workers, the local university, and the telephone company engaged together on one project)
- Feeling a sense of identity with those with whom one shares community

If the values of reciprocity, stewardship, responsibility, citizenship, civic virtue, and love describe various facets of how we take care of one another in a civil society, it matters a great deal whether we like, respect, trust, and understand one another or stereotype, distance, distort, and mistrust one another. Civil society stands or falls on this foundation of feelings. The magic of dialogue is that it really does enhance respect and acceptance of others. Without dialogue, people stereotype one another in a manner that prevents mutual understanding and acceptance. With dialogue, the stereotypes melt away, more often than not replaced by goodwill and deeper understanding.

The other way in which dialogue can civilize the Vision of the Free Market is more direct. An ideal use of dialogue is to reconcile conflicting systems of social values. What I have called the Vision of the Free Market and the Vision of Civil Society are high abstractions, remote from people's daily lives and concerns. It might be interesting intellectually, but it would not help much in practical terms, to have an elite group of social philosophers analyze the two visions, select their valid features, integrate them, and toss out the invalid ones. It would be a fascinating exercise, to be sure, but an academic one in the sense of failing to lead to action. Such exercises, I fear, would leave the larger culture unaffected.

Nor is the path of raw trial and error to be recommended. Too many things can go wrong. After making enough serious errors, getting back on the right track can prove impossible or come at the expense of generations of wasted lives and intolerable suffering (communism in Russia was one of the disastrous consequences of the trial-and-error approach to the mistakes of the Industrial Revolution). There is only one way the two visions can be reconciled pragmatically and realistically—through dialogue.

One of the many things dialogue can do is permit us to focus our imaginations on what kind of society we really want, relying on Arendt's process of representative thinking. Participants in such a dialogue would offer their unique perspectives on the two visions as they relate to their own everyday world of bringing up children properly, strengthening personal relationships with family and friends, pursuing happiness and quality of life, doing useful and self-fulfilling work, maintaining dignity and self-respect throughout life's vicissitudes, and keeping faith with beliefs that transcend the mundanities of everyday life.

When people engage one another, formally or informally, in dialogue about such concerns, they are seeking truths to live by, and through dialogue they have a good chance of finding them.

Conclusion

My friend social critic Lisbeth Schorr fears that I place too heavy a burden on dialogue. "My sense," she writes, "is that you are advocating a kind of exchange that is much more than talk—more than even the profound kind of talk represented by dialogue. It seems to me that a process that 'strengthens relationships and trust, forges alliances, finds truths that bind us together, and brings people into alignment on goals and strategies' would take work that goes well beyond talk."

This is a cogent criticism that I have pondered at length. Am I indeed expecting too much from mere talk, however special and disciplined it may be? Do we need to do a great deal of work over and above dialogue to achieve these kinds of results?

Upon reflection, I have concluded that at this particular juncture in history, I am not overstating the case for dialogue. My studies of the public reveal an immense pool of goodwill and good faith. People in the West are hungry for enhanced quality of life, for deeper community, for endowing our communal life with spiritual significance. In other words, they are *ready* to accomplish the goals I claim can be accomplished through dialogue. They are *ready* to accept truths over and above those of science and technical expertise without discarding their immense contributions. They are *ready* to meet on that ledge of dialogue of which Buber speaks in order to endow their own lives and those of others with a larger meaning.

As a policy wonk, I am all too aware of the heavy paraphernalia that ordinarily accompanies policies and action: laws and regulations, large outlays of capital, a high degree of organization, testing of results, moral and even physical coercion. As a society, we know about these things; we are adept in them. What we don't know very well, and where we are surprisingly awkward and not at all adept, is in the arts of listening with empathy, setting aside status differences, and examining with open minds the assumptions that underlie all the old scripts we all live by—in a word, dialogue.

At the risk of overstating the case, I believe that greater mastery of dialogue will advance our civility—and our civilization—a giant step forward. Dialogue has the magic to help us to do it.

Notes

Chapter 1: Overcoming the Dialogue Deficit

1. Interview with George Shultz on *The American Experience,* PBS, February 24, 1998.
2. I thank Marc Meringoff for bringing this reference to my attention.
3. William Butler Yeats, "The Second Coming," ll. 3–4, 7–8.

Chapter 2: What Makes Dialogue Unique?

1. Synthesized and adapted from the work of the Public Conversations Project, National Study Circles Resources, The Common Enterprise, Educators for Social Responsibility and Choice Point Consulting. Prepared for the Bipartisan Congressional Retreat by Mark Gerzon.
2. Howard Kirshenbaum and Valerie Land Henderson, eds. (Boston: Houghton Mifflin Company, 1989).
3. Ibid., p. 64.
4. See David Bohm, *On Dialogue,* Lee Nichol, ed. (London and New York: Routledge, 1996).
5. Ibid., pp. 7–12.

Chapter 5: Transforming Casual Encounters Through Dialogue

1. This incident is quoted in Lisbeth Schorr, *Common Purpose* (New York: Doubleday, 1977), p. 13, and amplified in conversation with the author.

Chapter 6: Planned Dialogue

1. Peter M. Senge *The Fifth Discipline: The Art and Practice of*

the Learning Organization (New York: Doubleday, 1994), p. 260.

2. Ibid., p. 265.

3. The philosopher Edmund Husserl used the term "bracketing assumptions" to refer to the process of provisionally taking one's own assumptions out of play. This is roughly what Senge and others mean by suspending one's assumptions.

4. My research suggests that Fishkin's concept of deliberation is too rationalistic and short term. People rarely change strongly held positions after a few hours of calm, reasonable conversation. When people do shift their views, it usually occurs over a period of months or years, after a stormy process of struggling with conflicting emotions and values. See Daniel Yankelovich, *Coming to Public Judgment* (Syracuse, N.Y.: Syracuse University Press, 1991).

Chapter 7: The Long and the Short of It

1. For a fuller account of the practice of sustained dialogue and the view of the world behind it, see Harold H. Saunders, *A Public Peace Process: Transforming Racial and Ethnic Conflict* (New York: St. Martin's Press, 1999).

2. Bohm, *On Dialogue*.

Chapter 8: Ten Potholes of the Mind

1. Daniel Yankelovich, *Coming to Public Judgment* (Syracuse, N.Y.: Syracuse University Press, 1991).

Chapter 9: Cultural Fault Lines

1. Clifford Geertz, "Blurred Genres: The Refiguration of Social Thought" in *Critical Theory Since 1965,* Hazard Adams and Leroy Searle, eds. (Tallahassee: University Press of Florida, 1986).

2. Survey by Princeton Survey Research Associates for *Newsweek,* June 19–25, 1995.

3. Survey by the Gallup Organization, May 9–12, 1996.

4. Takeo Doi, *The Anatomy of Dependence,* trans. John Bester (New York: Kodansha, 1973), p. 13.
5. Deborah Tannen, *You Just Don't Understand* (New York: Ballantine Books, 1991), pp. 17–18.
6. National Survey of 1,000 women eighteen years of age and older conducted by DYG for *Ladies' Home Journal,* May 1–12, 1997.
7. V. O. Key Jr., *Public Opinion and American Democracy* (New York: Knopf, 1961), p. 536.
8. Daniel Yankelovich, *Coming to Public Judgment* (Syracuse, N.Y.: Syracuse University Press, 1991).

Chapter 12: Dialogue as a Path to Public Judgment

1. Daniel Yankelovich, *Coming to Public Judgment* (Syracuse, N.Y.: Syracuse University Press, 1991).
2. Ibid., p. 16.

Chapter 13: From Expert Knowledge to Wisdom

1. When it entered the computer field some years later, the company dropped "Adding Machine" from its name.
2. Alasdair MacIntyre, *After Virtue: A Study in Moral Theory* (Notre Dame, Indiana; University of Notre Dame Press, 1987), p. 11.
3. Richard Bernstein, *The New Constellation* (Cambridge, Mass.: MIT Press, 1992), p. 4.
4. Richard Rorty, *Essays on Heidegger and Others* (Philosophical Papers, vol. 2) (Cambridge, England: Cambridge University Press, 1991), p. 1.
5. Richard Rorty, *Objectivity, Relativism, and Truth* (Philosophical Papers, vol. 1) (Cambridge, England: Cambridge University Press, 1991), p. 26. Uncomfortable with all dualisms, Rorty is suspicious of Habermas's distinction between scientific knowledge and the kind of knowledge gained through communicative action. He fears that Habermas is creating a new dualism. In my view, his fear is unfounded.

Habermas's effort to link types of knowledge with purpose is very much in the pragmatic tradition of treating ways of knowing as tools for coping with the world.

6. See, e.g., Howard Gardner, *The Mind's New Science* (New York: Basic Books, 1987) and *Multiple Intelligences* (New York: Basic Books, 1993).

Chapter 14: The Struggle for the Soul

1. Peter Schwartz and Peter Leyden, "The Long Boom," *Wired*, July 1997.
2. Ibid., p. 171.
3. David Potter, *People of Plenty: Economic Abundance and the American Character* (Chicago: University of Chicago Press, 1954), p. 69.
4. Arthur Okun, *Equality and Efficiency: The Big Tradeoff* (Washington, D.C.: Brookings Institute, 1975).
5. Benjamin R. Barber, "The Search for Civil Society," *The New Democrat*, March–April 1995, p. 13.
6. See the writings of Robert Putnam.
7. See the writings of Amitai Etzioni.

Resources

The following is a list of some of the organizations that work with the concept of dialogue.

Achieve Global
8875 Hidden River Parkway
Tampa, FL 33637-1034
Telephone: (813) 977-8875

Coherent Change Management
220 Palo Alto Avenue
San Francisco, CA 94114
Telephone: (415) 681-6488
E-mail: goldman@coherent.org

Common Ground Network for Life and Choice
1601 Connecticut Ave. N.W., Suite 200
Washington, DC 20009
Telephone: (202) 265-4300

Dialogos
929 Massachusetts Avenue
Cambridge, MA 02139
Telephone: (617) 576-7986

DiBianca-Berkman
546 Amwell Road
Neshanick, NJ 08853
Telephone: (908) 371-0969

The Health Forum
425 Market Street, 16th Floor
San Francisco, CA 94105
Telephone: (415) 356-4300

JMW
One Station Place
Stamford, CT 06902
Telephone: (203) 352-5000

Kettering Foundation
444 North Capitol Street N.W., Suite 434
Washington, DC 20001
Telephone: (202) 393-4478

Landmark Education Inc.
353 Sacramento Street, Suite 200
San Francisco, CA 94111
Telephone: (415) 616-2430

Mediators Foundation
9 Bowser Road
Lexington, MA 02420
Telephone: (303) 581-0294

Mediators Ltd.
3833 N. 57th Street
Boulder, CO 80301
Telephone: (303) 581-0294

San Diego Dialogue
UCSD-0176N
9500 Gilman Drive
La Jolla, CA 92093
Telephone: (619) 534-8408

Search for Common Ground
1601 Connecticut Ave. N.W., Suite 200
Washington, DC 20009
Telephone: (202) 265-4300
E-mail: search@sfcg.org

Society for Organizational Learning
222 Third Street, Suite 2323
Cambridge, MA 02142
Telephone: (617) 492-6260
Web site: www.sol-ne.org

Acknowledgments

Many friends and colleagues assisted me in thinking through the ideas and techniques for dialogue that fill the pages of this book. I wish to acknowledge their contribution and to thank them wholeheartedly for their willingness to read all or parts of the manuscript and give me their reactions—always supportive, sometimes too gentle, always helpful.

They include my colleagues at my firm, DYG Inc. (Madelyn Hochstein and George Pettinico), the Public Agenda (Deborah Wadsworth, Jean Johnson, Steve Farkas, Will Friedman, Margaret Dunning, Maurice Lazarus), the Kettering Foundation (David Mathews, Bob Kingston, Harold Saunders), Trinity Church (Dan Mathews, Maria Campbell, Fred Burnham, Deedee Taylor), Landmark Education (Barbara Holmes, Steve Zaffron), and UCSD (Mary Walshok, Chuck Nathanson).

They also include my friends Ann Overton, Rob Lehman, Marc Meringoff, Lisbeth Schorr, Sally Minard, Arthur White, Carole Hyatt, Leon Shapiro, Laurie Rosenblatt, Sandy Grieve, Dick McCormick, John Stern, John Immerwahr, Bill Gellerman, Rachel and Adam Bellow, Howard Hiatt, Maxine Wishner, my sister, Libby Schenkman, my agent, Ron Goldfarb, and my editor's assistant, Priscilla Holmes. All made perceptive observations and suggestions that greatly enhanced my understanding of how to present my subject.

My special gratitude goes to a handful of people who went far beyond friendship and obligation to assist me with every aspect of the book. Janice Kamrin, my friend and assistant, gave me invaluable help in ensuring that my abstract ideas were rendered concretely and in proper English. T George Harris gave me the benefit of his deep editorial experience and pushed me toward exploring the deeper meanings of dialogue. Norton Garfinckle helped me to present these materials in a more cogent fashion than they would otherwise have been. Fred Hills, my editor at Simon & Schuster, brought to bear his unerring instinct for the strengths and weaknesses of the text, gently guiding me toward revisions that vastly improved the book.

Finally, my loving friend and companion, Barbara Lee, read and reread every chapter and every revision, critiquing them with unerring intelligence and unstinting support when it was most needed.

Writing a book is partly a solitary affair and partly a product of dialogue with others. I have learned that, for myself at least, the very act of thinking is dependent on dialogue. Not only is this book about dialogue, it is itself a result of fruitful dialogue with the people listed above, and many others.

INDEX

facilitators, professional, 125–27, 145
facts and values, 24–26, 71, 179–80, 184–85, 188–94, 199–200
financial people, in meetings, 65
First Amendment, 26
First Knight, 43
Fishkin, James, 101–2
focus groups, 96–101, 105
  on education, 99–100
  optimal size of, 97
  purpose of, 96–97
  race and, 97–99
  stereotypes overcome in, 100–101
Four Ds, 36–46
  debate, 38–40
  discussion, 40–46
Free Market, Vision of, 201, 202–6, 207, 209, 212, 213, 215
Friedman, Maurice, 41

Gardner, Howard, 198
Geertz, Clifford, 151, 152
generalizing, from specific cases, 67–68, 128
Genesis, Book of, 165–66
Gergen, David, 35, 41
Germany, 211
Gerzon, Mark, 39
giving ground, 54
God, people's dialogic relationship with, 23
Gorbachev, Mikhail, 9
Grameen Bank, 192
Great Britain, 204
Grey, Maine, 104
group learning, 144–45

Habermas, Jürgen, 197
Halberstam, David, 180

Harvard Business School, 208
Harvard University, 11, 177
health care, 68–70, 138, 152
Healthcare Forum, 36
Hebrew mysticism, 23
"heroic medicine," 138
holding back, 130–31
Homebuilders, 79
Houston, Tex., 68
humanities-sciences gap, 153
Hussein, Saddam, 166

I and Thou (Buber), 14–15
Iceland, 9
Ideas, Platonic, 195
I-It relationships, 149–52, 157
individualism, 207–8
individual training, 143–44
influentials, 155
information, wisdom compared with, 191–92
Institute for Educational Leadership, 102
intelligence, multiple forms of, 198
Internet, 159, 163, 164
investments, pension funds and, 47–51, 53, 66
Iraq, 166
Isaacs, William, 23, 36, 110–12, 113–14, 117
"Is it good for the Jews?," 141
Israel, 9–10, 114
issues books, 102, 138
I-Thou relationships, 14–15, 23, 42, 88, 108, 113, 149–50, 154, 157

Japanese:
  courtesy shown guests by, 153
  in meetings, 65